EYEWITNESS
WONDERS OF THE WORLD

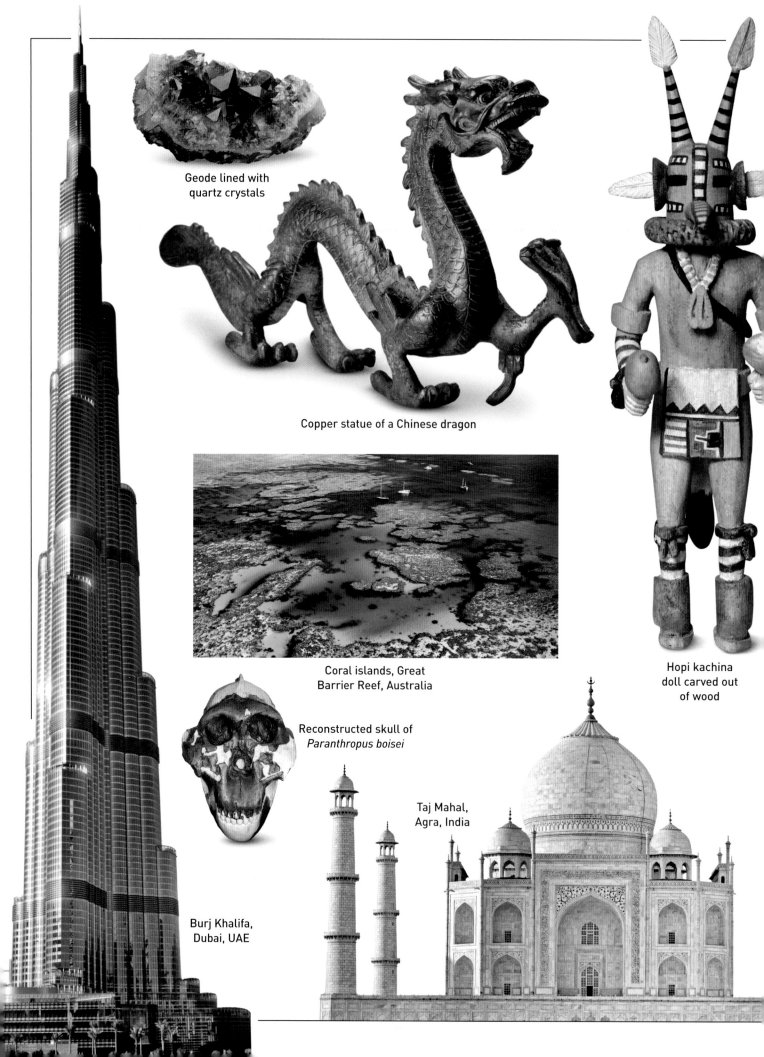

Geode lined with
quartz crystals

Copper statue of a Chinese dragon

Coral islands, Great
Barrier Reef, Australia

Reconstructed skull of
Paranthropus boisei

Hopi kachina
doll carved out
of wood

Taj Mahal,
Agra, India

Burj Khalifa,
Dubai, UAE

Palmato
gecko

EYEWITNESS
WONDERS OF
THE WORLD

Written by
TOM JACKSON

The pyramids of Giza, Egypt

Crown-of-thorns starfish

Gold image of Inti

Statue of David Livingstone

Penguin Random House

Consultants   John Woodward, Philip Parker

DK DELHI
Project editor   Bharti Bedi
Project art editor   Nishesh Batnagar
Editorial team   Ishani Nandi, Priyaneet Singh, Suneha Dutta
Design team   Amit Varma, Deep Shikha Walia,
Isha Nagar, Nidhi Mehra, Shreya Sadhan
Senior editor   Shatarupa Chaudhuri
Senior DTP designers   Harish Aggarwal, Jagtar Singh
DTP designer   Pawan Kumar
Pre-production manager   Balwant Singh
Managing editor   Alka Thakur
Managing art editor   Romi Chakraborty
Production manager   Pankaj Sharma
Senior picture researcher   Sumedha Chopra
Jacket editorial manager   Saloni Talwar
Jacket designers   Dhirendra Singh, Suhita Dharamjit

DK LONDON
Editor   Ashwin Khurana
US editor   Margaret Parrish
Senior art editor   Rachael Grady
Managing editor   Gareth Jones
Managing art editor   Philip Letsu
Publisher   Andrew Macintyre
Senior pre-producer   Luca Frassinetti
Senior producer   Charlotte Cade
Jacket editor   Maud Whatley
Jacket designer   Laura Brim
Jacket design development manager   Sophia MTT
Publishing director   Jonathan Metcalf
Associate publishing director   Liz Wheeler
Art director   Phil Ormerod

First American Edition, 2014
Published in the United States by DK Publishing
1450 Broadway, Suite 801,
New York, NY 10018

19 10
014-265424—07/14

ISBN: 978-1-4654-2249-1 (Paperback)
ISBN: 978-1-4654-2250-7 (ALB)

DK books are available at special discounts when purchased
in bulk for sales promotions, premiums, fund-raising, or educational
use. For details, contact: DK Publishing Special Markets, 1450 Broadway,
Suite 801, New York, NY 10018 or SpecialSale@dk.com.

Printed in China

A WORLD OF IDEAS;
SEE ALL THERE IS TO KNOW
www.dk.com

Andean flamingos

Eiffel Tower, Paris, France

Contents

Moai statues,
Easter Island,
Chile

Mount Everest

The highest place on Earth, the summit (or peak) of Mount Everest rises 29,029 ft (8,848 m) above sea level. The climb to the top—a patch of rock and snow no bigger than a double bed—is long and dangerous. So far, around 3,500 climbers have succeeded in reaching the summit.

Mount Everest is located on the border between Nepal and China.

Scaling the peak

In 1953, New Zealander Edmund Hillary (left) and Tenzing Norgay (right), from Nepal, became the first people to reach the top of Mount Everest. They carried extra oxygen in canisters to help them breathe as they went up.

Tough terrain

The air at the top of Mount Everest contains only a third of the oxygen it has at ground level. Winds blow at up to 110 mph (180 kph) and temperatures can drop to −80°F (−62°C). Rescue helicopters cannot risk flying at such high altitudes, so injured climbers have to be carried down to safety.

The Himalayas

The world's highest mountain range, the Himalayas are about 10 million years old. Formed by gradual movements in the Earth's crust, the Himalayas are, in fact, still rising: Mount Everest "grows" 2 in (5 cm) each year!

Prayer flags at Rongbuk Monastery

Highest monastery
Located halfway up the northern side of the mountain, Rongbuk Monastery is the world's highest monastery, at 16,340 ft (4,980 m). According to Tibetan Buddhist beliefs, goddess Miyolangsangma lives at the top of the mountain. Many climbers seek her blessing before starting their expedition.

Sherpas
The Sherpas are a group of people who live in the valleys around the mountain. They earn their living as guides and porters carrying equipment for visiting climbers. The world-famous Tenzing Norgay was a Sherpa.

Sherpas can carry massive loads

Glimpses of the past
The limestone that forms the top section of Mount Everest contains fossilized seashells and remains of various sea animals. These fossils show us that the rock—now the highest point on Earth—formed at the bottom of the ocean around 450 million years ago.

Ammonite shell fossil

There is a permanent cover of snow at higher altitudes

Mount Everest was named in 1865 after George Everest, a British surveyor

Tin can used to make the turtle's head

Gas tank forms the back

Art from trash
The trail leading to Mount Everest is littered with garbage left behind by careless climbers. In 2012, 1.5 tons (1.4 metric tons) of litter was collected, some of which was made into art—including this turtle.

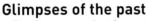

7

Mount Roraima

Mount Roraima stands where the borders of Venezuela, Brazil, and Guyana meet in South America.

A 2-billion-year-old flat-topped mountain, Mount Roraima is in the middle of the South American grasslands. "Roraima" means "the great blue-green" in the language of the Pemon people, who have lived here for thousands of years. The Pemon rarely climb to the top of the mountain because they believe that the spirits of their ancestors live there.

First report
The English explorer Walter Raleigh came to the area in 1596 in search of treasure. He provided the first official record of Mount Roraima, although he never climbed to the top himself.

Tabletop mountain
The Pemon people use the word *tepui* (meaning "house of the gods") to refer to the region's tabletop mountains, which have near-vertical sides and a flat surface. At 9,219 ft (2,810 m), Mount Roraima is the highest *tepui* in the area. Heavy rainfall on the mountain's surface flows over its 1,312-ft- (400-m-) steep cliff faces, creating some of the highest waterfalls on Earth.

Sandstone carved into a turtlelike shape

Alien landscape
Mount Roraima is mostly made of hard sandstone that has been worn away by daily rainfall and constant winds over millions of years. These harsh conditions can create unusual rock formations, such as the "turtle rock" (shown here).

Crystal valley

The Valley of Crystals is a small water channel carved into the top of the mountain. Over time, the water has worn away the sandstone surface, exposing the pinkish white quartz beneath. As a result, quartz crystals now line the valley floor like a bed of jewels.

Predator plants

There is very little soil on top of Mount Roraima. To survive in a place without the essential nutrients found in soil, some native plants, such as this sundew, trap insects for food. Bright drops of a sticky liquid at the ends of the plant's tendrils attract and trap mosquitoes and other bugs. After the plant catches the insect, its leaves close around the prey and digest it.

Sticky liquid on a sundew's spiked leaves traps insects

Black skin helps this toad hide among dark rocks

Roraima bush toad

The Roraima bush toad is found only on Mount Roraima. The species has been cut off from the world for a long time—its closest relative lives in Africa. This proves that the mountain was formed millions of years ago, when Africa and South America were still joined together.

Roraima bush toad

The lost world

Mount Roraima was the inspiration for Arthur Conan Doyle's novel *The Lost World*. Published in 1912, the book tells the story of a group of explorers who climb onto a high, vast plateau hidden by the clouds. Here, they find a land inhabited by dinosaurs and other prehistoric creatures.

THE LOST WORLD

A RIPPING TALE GUARDIAN

ARTHUR CONAN DOYLE

Mount Fuji

The highest peak in Japan, Mount Fuji is so large that it can be seen from the city of Tokyo 60 miles (100 km) away. Noted for its great beauty, Mount Fuji is held sacred by the Shinto religion. Although this active volcano last erupted in 1707, scientists believe it will erupt again.

Mount Fuji is in the southeast of Honshu, Japan's largest island.

Fire festival
Each summer, the people of Yoshida, a town at the foot of Mount Fuji, light bamboo torches to honor the goddess of the mountain. They believe that this ritual will prevent eruptions and keep climbers safe.

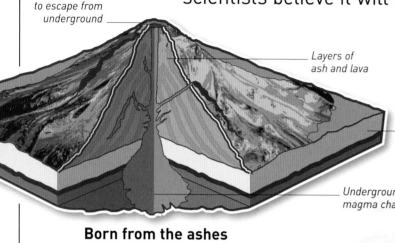

Crater allows lava and gases to escape from underground

Layers of ash and lava

Earth's crust is broken into sections, or plates

Underground magma chamber

Activity in crater is recorded by scientists to predict the next eruption

Born from the ashes
Mount Fuji is a stratovolcano—a cone-shaped volcano formed by layers of lava and volcanic ash. The lava comes from a magma (molten rock) chamber that lies beneath Mount Fuji where three parts of the Earth's crust meet.

An explosive past
There has been volcanic activity in this area for millions of years. Mount Fuji is the third volcano to have formed here, burying what was left of two older ones. At 10,000 years old, it is quite young for a mountain. When Mount Fuji last erupted, it ripped an enormous second crater in the side of the mountain.

Shrines

There are 1,300 Shinto shrines in Japan, where people worship the spirits of volcanoes. The most important of these shrines are around Mount Fuji.

Decorative spires at the top of the shrine

Cherry blossoms

The cherry blossom is the symbol of the Shinto goddess Konohana Sakuya Hime, who worshippers believe lives on Mount Fuji. Many Japanese families celebrate spring by having a picnic under the trees—a tradition called *hanami*.

Natural beauty

Mount Fuji's symmetrical cone makes the mountain look almost the same from every direction. Katsushika Hokusai potrayed the mountain in a collection of woodblock prints called *36 Views of Mount Fuji*.

"Fuji from Kanaya on the Tokaido road," by Katsushika Hokusai

To the top

In summer, about 300,000 people climb to the 12,389-ft (3,776-m) peak. Visitors travel half the way by bus, then walk to the top—a journey of four hours. Many climb at night so they can watch the sunrise from the peak.

Old Faithful

The most famous geyser in the world, Old Faithful, is so called because it is both regular and predictable. It is one of 200 geysers in Yellowstone National Park, which also features hot springs, boiling mud pools, and fumaroles (outlets that let out steam and other gases).

Old Faithful is located in Yellowstone National Park, Wyoming.

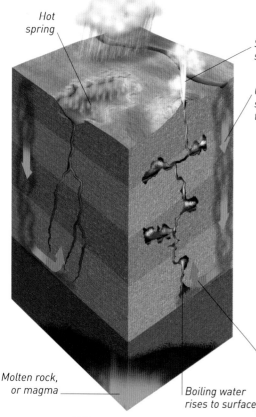

Hot spring

Spray of water and steam from the geyser

Groundwater seeps down through rocks

Molten rock, or magma

Boiling water rises to surface

Water is heated when it comes in contact with hot rocks

Up to 8,500 gallons (32,000 liters) of water is squirted 185 ft (56 m) into the sky

Right on time!
Old Faithful erupts every 91 minutes, on average, and the displays generally last 2–3 minutes. However, Old Faithful has slowed down since its discovery in 1870, when it used to erupt every 65 minutes. The longer interval may be the result of a change in the underground water levels due to earthquakes in the region.

What is a geyser?
A geyser is a spring that releases hot water and steam from the ground. Beneath Old Faithful is a deep underground reservoir containing boiling water heated to almost 400°F (200°C) by magma (molten rocks). This water regularly surges to the surface through a crack leading to the geyser and erupts as a fountain.

Cone shape of the geyser directs a steady spray of water

Old Faithful Inn
Yellowstone National Park receives more than 3 million visitors a year. Most tour the park by bus or car. Some of the best views of Old Faithful, however, are from a nearby hotel, which has been hosting tourists for more than a century.

Old-fashioned bus on a park tour

General Sheridan (center) with his soldiers

Nature's laundry
In 1882, US soldiers—under the command of General Philip Sheridan and stationed in the park—discovered that the geyser served as a natural washing machine. When the geyser was quiet, they threw their laundry into the water, and the clothes were spat out by the next eruption, thoroughly cleaned!

First national park
In 1872, Yellowstone became the first national park in the world. It is called so after the Native American name for the main river in the park, *Mi tse a-da-zi*, meaning "rock yellow".

Yellowstone River flows through the Grand Canyon of Yellowstone

Giant Prismatic Spring
The Giant Prismatic Spring in Yellowstone National Park is the largest hot spring in the US. The bright bands of color in the spring are produced by bacteria that grow in hot water.

The Dead Sea

Nestled in the mountains between Israel and Jordan, the Dead Sea is 31 miles (50 km) long and 9 miles (15 km) wide. The Dead Sea is, in fact, a lake—one of the saltiest on Earth. Its surface lies 1,400 ft (427 m) below sea level, making its shoreline the lowest patch of dry land on Earth.

The Dead Sea lies between Israel, Jordan, and Palestine.

Salt content

Water flows into the Dead Sea from the Jordan River. The water gets trapped in the lake and evaporates in the fierce heat of the Sun, leaving salt crystals behind on the shore.

Asphalt

The Dead Sea releases a material called asphalt—an oily, solid form of petroleum—through cracks in its seabed. Lumps of asphalt can be seen floating on the lake's surface.

Water here is almost 10 times saltier than that of the ocean

Floating away

The lake's water is very dense because it contains so much salt. It is much denser than the human body, allowing swimmers to float around effortlessly on the surface.

Mineral wealth

The southern part of the lake contains shallow pools where the water evaporates, leaving behind minerals such as bromine. This unusual red-brown liquid is used in fire-retardants, which stop things from burning.

The Dead Sea refinery at Sidom, Israel, harvests bromine from the water

A sinkhole near the Dead Sea

Dead Sea dying?

Much of the ground around the lake is drying out and collapsing into sinkholes—holes that can open up suddenly as a result of erosion. To keep the Dead Sea from shrinking, nearby countries have agreed to build a 110-mile (177-km) pipeline to bring in extra water from the Red Sea, which is located between Africa and Asia.

Ink made from soot of burned olive oil

Ancient secrets

In 1946, a shepherd discovered ancient parchments in a cave at Qumran by the Dead Sea. It is thought that the 972 "Dead Sea Scrolls" found in the area were written as far back as 400 BCE by members of a Jewish sect called the Essenes.

Parchment from the Dead Sea Scrolls

Swimmers need to be careful to keep the salty, stinging water out of their eyes

Dead Sea mud pack helps cleanse the skin

Health benefits

Rich in minerals, the Dead Sea's water and mud are believed to ease pain in muscles and joints. Breathing the air above the lake is also thought to have health benefits, since it is free of pollen and other particles that cause allergies such as hay fever.

The Grand Canyon

The spectacular Grand Canyon was cut into the desert rocks by the Colorado River. The canyon is so wide that an entire city could fit between its rims; it is so deep that the world's tallest building could fit inside it twice.

The Grand Canyon is in a high desert region of northern Arizona.

Mule mail

There are no roads in the Grand Canyon, just steep, rocky tracks. Mules are used for transportation and also for carrying mail. Supai, a village deep inside the canyon, is the only place in the United States where the mail still arrives by mule.

Mule delivery along a canyon trail

Pueblo peoples

Native American Pueblo peoples have lived in the canyon for 3,000 years. They are thought to be the ancestors of the Hopi tribe that currently live there. The canyon's oldest structures are the 900-year-old food stores cut into the cliffs by the natives. In 1540, Spanish explorer García López de Cárdenas became the first outsider to visit the canyon.

Hopi kachina doll carved out of wood

Rocks exposed at the bottom of the canyon are nearly 2 billion years old

Colorado River

Skywalk extends out 70 ft (21 m) from the canyon wall

About 120 people can stand on the Skywalk at a time

Risk takers

In 2013, American acrobat Nik Wallenda walked 1,400 ft (427 m) on a high wire suspended 1,500 ft (457 m) above the canyon floor. In 1999, another stunt performer, Robbie Knievel, jumped across the canyon on a motorcycle.

Skywalk

Shaped like a horseshoe, with a see-through floor, the Skywalk bridge allows tourists to stand 4,000 ft (1,220 m) above the Colorado River. More than 4 million tourists visit the canyon every year. While most come to enjoy the view, some hike to the bottom or take thrilling helicopter rides.

Animals and plants

The Grand Canyon is home to several plants and animals that exist nowhere else. The Kaibab squirrel is unique to the area and lives mainly in the canyon's northern forests. There are also six species of fish that exist only in the canyon's rivers. Commonly found animals, such as mule deer and bighorn sheep, live mainly on the south side of the canyon.

Broad, feathery tail

The canyon

A canyon is a deep valley with steep sides, usually with a river flowing through it. Created over 3 million years, the Grand Canyon was formed when the land around it was pushed upward, and the Colorado River cut through many layers of rock. It is 277 miles (446 km) long, up to 18 miles (29 km) wide, and about 1 mile (1.6 km) deep.

Uluru

Uluru lies near the center of Australia, close to the city of Alice Springs.

Sacred to the Aboriginal people of Australia, Uluru, or Ayers Rock, is the world's largest rock. It has a circumference of 5.8 miles (9.4 km) and is 1,142 ft (348 m) tall at its highest point. Hundreds of tourists visit the rock every day to tour around the base and to view the Aboriginal rock art sites in the region.

Kata Tjuta

Kata Tjuta is a cluster of 36 domes of rock, the highest of which is 656 ft (200 m) taller than Uluru. On the surface, Kata Tjuta lies about 16 miles (25 km) from Uluru, but the two rock formations are linked underground.

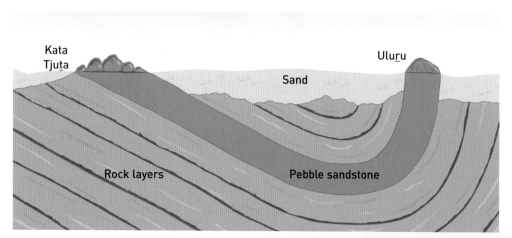

Kata Tjuta

Uluru

Sand

Rock layers

Pebble sandstone

Concealed connections

Uluru and Kata Tjuta are the two ends of a thick rock layer. At ground level, Uluru rises as a huge single dome, whereas the pebble-filled rock of Kata Tjuta has been worn away into several sections.

The rock

Made up of a sandstone called arkose, Uluru gets its red color from iron-rich minerals in the rock. As the angle of the Sun changes through the day, the rock can look red, orange, yellow, or gray.

Uluru turns a deep orange-yellow at sunrise and sunset

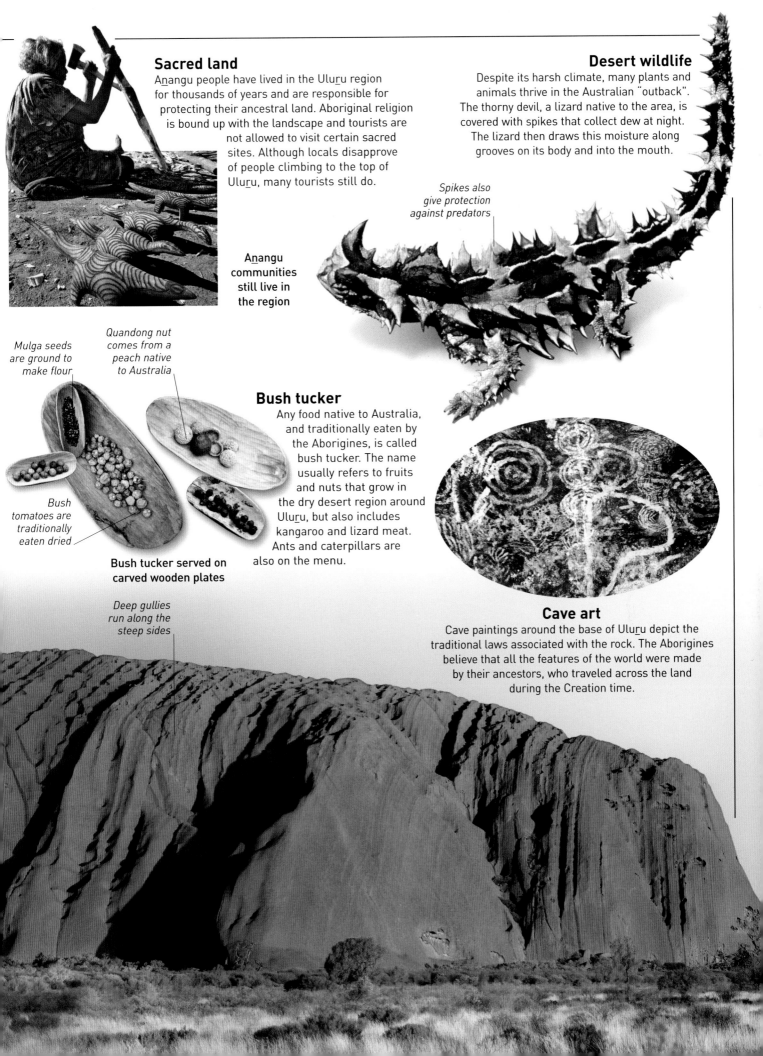

Sacred land

Anangu people have lived in the Uluru region for thousands of years and are responsible for protecting their ancestral land. Aboriginal religion is bound up with the landscape and tourists are not allowed to visit certain sacred sites. Although locals disapprove of people climbing to the top of Uluru, many tourists still do.

Anangu communities still live in the region

Desert wildlife

Despite its harsh climate, many plants and animals thrive in the Australian "outback". The thorny devil, a lizard native to the area, is covered with spikes that collect dew at night. The lizard then draws this moisture along grooves on its body and into the mouth.

Spikes also give protection against predators

Mulga seeds are ground to make flour

Quandong nut comes from a peach native to Australia

Bush tomatoes are traditionally eaten dried

Bush tucker

Any food native to Australia, and traditionally eaten by the Aborigines, is called bush tucker. The name usually refers to fruits and nuts that grow in the dry desert region around Uluru, but also includes kangaroo and lizard meat. Ants and caterpillars are also on the menu.

Bush tucker served on carved wooden plates

Cave art

Cave paintings around the base of Uluru depict the traditional laws associated with the rock. The Aborigines believe that all the features of the world were made by their ancestors, who traveled across the land during the Creation time.

Deep gullies run along the steep sides

The Cave of Crystals

The Naica Mine, in Mexico, is famous for its beautiful crystal caves. The most spectacular of these is the Cave of Crystals, which houses the biggest crystals in the world. In 2000, two brothers accidentally discovered this cave while drilling an underground tunnel to look for lead ore.

The Cave of Crystals is in Chihuahua, a state in northern Mexico.

Crystal palace

The Cave of Crystals is a limestone cavern. Most of its crystals are at least 20 ft (6 m) long, while the largest discovered here, so far, is twice that size and weighs 55 tons (50 metric tons). Only a handful of explorers are allowed in the cave to study these fragile crystals.

Explorers wear rubber boots, because they must make sure not to damage the soft crystals

Cave of Swords

Named after its daggerlike crystals, the Cave of Swords was found near the surface of the Naica Mine in 1910. It contains crystals similar to—though smaller than—those found in the Cave of Crystals.

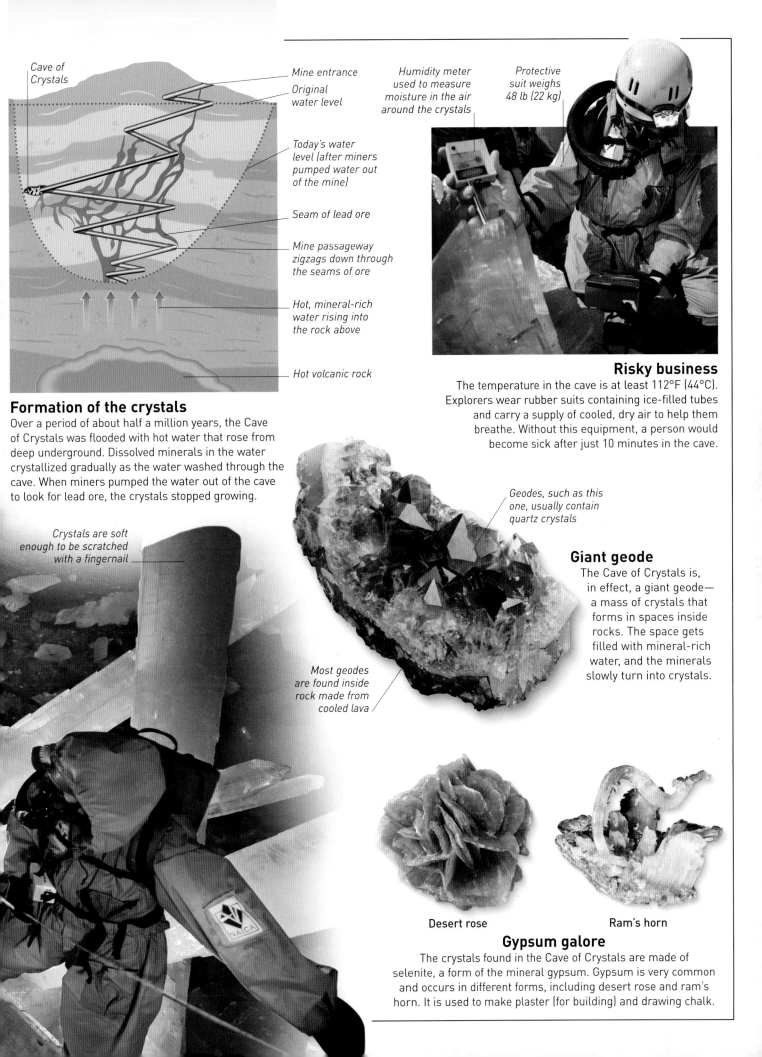

Cave of Crystals

Mine entrance

Original water level

Today's water level (after miners pumped water out of the mine)

Seam of lead ore

Mine passageway zigzags down through the seams of ore

Hot, mineral-rich water rising into the rock above

Hot volcanic rock

Formation of the crystals

Over a period of about half a million years, the Cave of Crystals was flooded with hot water that rose from deep underground. Dissolved minerals in the water crystallized gradually as the water washed through the cave. When miners pumped the water out of the cave to look for lead ore, the crystals stopped growing.

Humidity meter used to measure moisture in the air around the crystals

Protective suit weighs 48 lb (22 kg)

Risky business

The temperature in the cave is at least 112°F (44°C). Explorers wear rubber suits containing ice-filled tubes and carry a supply of cooled, dry air to help them breathe. Without this equipment, a person would become sick after just 10 minutes in the cave.

Crystals are soft enough to be scratched with a fingernail

Geodes, such as this one, usually contain quartz crystals

Giant geode

The Cave of Crystals is, in effect, a giant geode— a mass of crystals that forms in spaces inside rocks. The space gets filled with mineral-rich water, and the minerals slowly turn into crystals.

Most geodes are found inside rock made from cooled lava

Desert rose

Ram's horn

Gypsum galore

The crystals found in the Cave of Crystals are made of selenite, a form of the mineral gypsum. Gypsum is very common and occurs in different forms, including desert rose and ram's horn. It is used to make plaster (for building) and drawing chalk.

Salar de Uyuni

The largest salt flat in the world, Salar de Uyuni stretches across an area of 4,086 sq miles (10,582 sq km)—10 times the size of Los Angeles—and is covered in a 3-ft- (1-m-) thick crust of salt. It is also the world's flattest place, with less than 3 ft (1 m) between its highest and lowest points.

Salar de Uyuni lies on the Altiplano, a high plateau in Bolivia, South America.

Isla Pabellón, one of the highest islands in Salar de Uyuni

Landlocked islands

The rocky islands rising above the salt are the peaks of ancient volcanoes that were once submerged under a huge prehistoric lake. With little rainfall and no other major source of water nearby, the lake dried out about 15,000 years ago, exposing the peaks we see today.

Life in the desert

Plants cannot survive on the salt flats. However, hardy shrubs and cacti grow on the rocky islands, where they provide food for animals such as the large, rabbitlike rodents called viscachas.

Viscachas live in large groups known as colonies

Visual delights

Each year, the monsoon rains flood the salt flat, turning it into a vast pool. The still water creates such perfect reflections that it is difficult to tell where the ground stops and the sky begins.

Flock together

Large flocks of flamingos fly to Salar de Uyuni every November and gather by shallow pools to raise their young. The birds lay eggs in nests made from mounds of mud. When the eggs hatch, the adults feed their chicks tiny shrimp that thrive in the salty water.

Andean flamingos in flight

The great salt flats

Salar de Uyuni fills a hollow basin surrounded by the Andes Mountains. Rain and floodwater get trapped in the area because there is nowhere for it to go. Over time, the water evaporates, leaving behind deposits of salt and other minerals.

Layer of dry salt cracks into hexagon "tiles"

Mineral mine

Salar de Uyuni contains about 10.8 billion tons (9.8 billion metric tons) of salt—27,500 tons (25,000 metric tons) of which is mined for use in cooking every year. Miners dig through the solid crust to reach a wet, salty mush called brine. Valuable minerals are extracted from the brine, including the metal lithium, used in rechargeable batteries.

Salt hotels

Visitors can stay in salt hotels, where all the furniture is made of blocks of salt. When it rains, the salt mixes with the water and gets washed away, so regular repairs are needed.

The Serengeti

The Serengeti covers an area of 12,000 sq miles (30,000 sq km) across the border between Kenya and Tanzania.

Known locally as "the land that goes on forever," the Serengeti is a wide open plain in East Africa. Every year, more than a million animals make a long journey known as the Great Migration, which attracts many tourists. People also go on a safari or visit other attractions such as the Ngorongoro Crater.

The vast plains

The Serengeti is a savanna—a mixture of grassland and scattered trees—with woods and wetlands. The eastern part gets the least rain and is covered in short grasses. Moving west, the rainfall increases and taller grasses grow there. Farther west, the grassland becomes a thorny woodland, and then a wetland where it meets Lake Victoria.

Acacia trees provide shade and food for many animals

Zebras eat dry, tough grasses, while the wildebeest eat the soft grasses left behind

As old as time

On the eastern edge of the Serengeti is the Olduvai Gorge. Fossil bones and stone tools found here tell us that hominids—the ancient relatives of humans—lived in the area around 2 million years ago. Two hominid species lived in the gorge—*Paranthropus boisei* and *Homo habilis*.

Skull of *Paranthropus boisei* reconstructed using 1.75-million-year-old fossil fragments from Olduvai Gorge

Male wildebeest can have horns up to 32 in (80 cm) long

Great Migration

Every year, 1.2 million wildebeest make a 500-mile (800-km) journey across the Serengeti. In the spring, the wildebeest give birth to calves in the eastern grasslands. By May, the grass begins to run out, and the herds move to the western wetlands in search of food and water. When these wetlands dry up in July, the wildebeest go north, where it continues to rain. In winter, they head back east, and the cycle begins again.

Predator alert!
A quarter of the animals making the Great Migration die on the journey, many of them killed by lions, leopards, or hyenas. The spotted hyena is a fierce predator. It usually hunts in packs to bring down large prey, but can also hunt alone. Its jaws are strong enough to crack bone.

Spotted hyena with its prey

Traditional Maasai jewelry

People
The people of the Serengeti are called the Maasai. They are nomads, which means they do not have a permanent home. Instead, they move regularly, taking their cattle herds to new grazing areas. The main source of income for the Maasai is selling livestock, which includes cattle, goats, and sheep.

Volcanic neighbors
The Ngorongoro Crater is located in the volcanic mountains along the eastern end of the Serengeti. At 12½ miles (20 km) wide, it is one of the largest volcanic craters in the world and was formed when a volcano erupted about 2 million years ago. The crater is now a haven for wildlife such as zebras, cheetahs, and flamingos. In the rainy season, the crater fills with water, forming Lake Magadi.

Maasai man in ceremonial garb

The Namib Desert

One of the harshest deserts in the world, the Namib Desert stretches across 1,250 miles (2,000 km). It features some of the world's highest dunes, along with dried-up marshes and a rocky coast. The red sand of the Namib is about 80 million years old, making the desert one of the oldest on Earth.

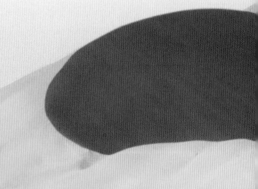

The Namib Desert is situated along the southwest coast of Africa.

Drinking in
The palmato gecko can only be found in the Namib Desert. Since it has no eyelids, the gecko uses its long tongue to clean its eyes. It also uses its tongue to "drink" condensed fog from its eyes to help it survive in the dry conditions.

Sun scorches the wood, blackening it

Dead marsh
Surrounded by massive dunes, Deadvlei (meaning "dead marsh") was once a desert oasis. It was formed when the Tsauchab River flooded the region, creating shallow pools that allowed the camelthorn trees to grow. All that remains today is dry clay and dead tree trunks.

The red dunes
The dunes in the desert's Sossusvlei region are some of the highest in the world. Among the most famous are the Big Daddy (1,066 ft/325 m high) and Dune 7 (1,257 ft/383 m high). The dunes are formed by red iron-rich sand and range from orange to red.

Desert elephants

African elephants can survive in the Namib Desert because they have adapted to its harsh, dry climate. They keep cool by coating themselves with sand and can go for days without water, surviving on the moisture in their food. Sometimes they make long journeys at night to reach watering holes.

Leaves grow up to 13 ft (4 m) long

Large feet make it easier to walk on sand

Against all odds

The Welwitschia, which is only found in this area, grows near the coast. The plant grows by trapping moisture from the sea fog through its leaves and can survive for more than 1,000 years. It has just two leaves, which get shredded by the strong winds.

Shipwreck on the Skeleton Coast

Skeleton Coast

The shoreline of the Namib Desert, the Skeleton Coast, is known for its heavy surf and sea fog. It gets its name from the skeletons of sea animals and remains of shipwrecks. Ships lose their way in the thick fog and are wrecked on the offshore rocks. The local people nicknamed this coast "the land God made in anger."

Dune in Sossusvlei at sunset

The Giant Forest

Some of the world's largest trees grow on the mountain slopes of central California. Standing 6,000 ft (1,829 m) above sea level, the Giant Forest is home to towering giant sequoia trees—the largest living things on Earth.

The Giant Forest is part of the Sequoia National Park in California.

Grove of giants

The Giant Forest is one of 68 patches of forest in California where giant sequoias grow. Five of the largest trees in the world—General Sherman, General Grant, President, Lincoln, and Franklin—are found here.

Colossal trees

Giant sequoias can grow to 310 ft (94.8 m) tall and 49,500 cubic ft (1,400 cubic m) in volume, and can live more than 3,000 years. The President, a 246-ft- (75-m-) tall giant sequoia, is around 3,200 years old.

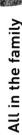

Small beginnings

Each year, the larger sequoias grow up to 11,000 cones, which release around 300,000 seeds. Each seed is only 1/8 in (4 mm) long and has tiny wings.

All in the family

Although they are closely related, coastal redwoods in California are much taller than giant sequoias, growing up to 330 ft (100 m). A tunnel cut through a coastal redwood is wide enough to accommodate a car, as seen in the Chandelier Tree in California's Drive-Thru Tree Park.

President, the third largest tree in the world, with a volume of 45,167 cubic ft (1,279 cubic m)

Forest ecologist climbs up to measure the tree's height

Safety first

Wildfires can spread quickly in summer. Forest fire teams burn any dead wood and dry leaves before they catch fire in order to protect the wildlife and nearby communities.

Record breakers

Human	Giraffe	General Sherman	Lindsey Creek (died in 1905)
6 ft (1.8 m)	18 ft (5.5 m)	274.9 ft (83.8 m)	390 ft (118.9 m)

The largest living tree by volume is the giant sequoia General Sherman, with a volume of 52,508 cubic ft (1,487 cubic m). The tallest living tree is Hyperion, a coastal redwood at 379.3 ft (115.6 m). The biggest tree on record was Lindsey Creek, a coastal redwood with a volume of 90,052 cubic ft (2,550 cubic m).

Circle of life

A tree's age can be determined by the number of rings on its trunk. Every season, a tree produces new layers of wood around the trunk. Each layer looks slightly different, which makes it possible to count and study the rings. These giant trees started growing centuries ago. The rings on this coastal redwood in Muir Woods, California, show that it was 1,021 years old.

1930: The tree falls

1908: Muir Woods National Monument established

1776: US Declaration of Independence

1492: Columbus sails to the Americas

1325: The Aztec begin construction of Tenochtitlán, Mexico

909 CE: The tree is born

27 ft (8.2 m) wide at the base

Great Barrier Reef

The Great Barrier Reef runs through the western end of the Coral Sea.

Stretching along the northeastern coast of Australia, the Great Barrier Reef is the world's largest structure made by living organisms. At 1,600 miles (2,600 km) long, the reef forms a strip of bright turquoise that is so large it can be seen from space.

In the shallows
Coral has been growing along the Australian coast for 25 million years, but the current reef is about 7,000 years old. The Great Barrier Reef measures 500 ft (150 m) at its deepest point and consists of around 3,000 individual coral reefs.

Animal life
The reef is home to thousands of marine animals, including six species of turtle, 17 species of sea snake, 1,500 types of fish, and dozens of different kinds of sharks. The moray eel is one of the reef's most ferocious hunters. It hides among the coral until it is time to find its next meal.

Staghorn coral grows in branches

The reef
Coral reefs are made up of the skeletons of corals. Each piece of coral is formed from thousands of tiny animals called polyps. Many polyps have hard cases, which are left behind when they die. New polyps grow on top of these skeletons, and the rocky reef gradually builds up, at about ½ in (1 cm) a year.

Soft corals look more like seaweed

Stony coral releases bundles of cells into the water

Dangerous pest

The crown-of-thorns starfish eats the soft parts of coral. It turns its stomach inside out to engulf its prey. Hungry swarms of these starfish can kill large parts of the reef, which often take years to recover.

Coral spawning

Corals spawn (produce young) by releasing male and female reproductive cells into the water. These combine to form baby corals, which can swim. Once a year, entire colonies of coral spawn at the same time, releasing great clouds of cells into the water at night.

Crown-of-thorns starfish has up to 21 arms

Bright light helps the divers to see reef's colors

Tentacles help collect food particles

Exploration and research

Most of the Great Barrier Reef is a protected area called a marine reserve. Marine biologists study the marine life and make sure human activities are not damaging the reef.

Underwater video camera

Making food

Coral polyps use their tentacles to gather food particles, but they also get food from microscopic, plantlike algae that live inside their bodies. These algae produce sugar, which they share with the polyps.

Victoria Falls

Measuring 328 ft (100 m) high and 5,597 ft (1,706 m) wide, Victoria Falls is the world's biggest sheet of falling water, when the river is in full flow. Its traditional African name is Mosi-oa-Tunya, which means "the smoke that thunders."

Victoria Falls forms the border between Zambia and Zimbabwe in southern Africa.

Bungee platform on a railroad bridge at a height of 420 ft (128 m)

In the Queen's name
In 1855, Scottish explorer David Livingstone became the first European to view this waterfall when he spotted it from an island in the middle of the river. He named it after the British monarch Queen Victoria.

Extreme sports
The waterfall is a major destination for adventure sports. A railroad bridge close to Victoria Falls serves as a perfect site for bungee jumping. Thrill-seekers can also zip across the water, suspended from a cable between the craggy cliffs, or navigate rafts through the Zambezi River's ferocious rapids.

The falls
Following the November rains, the Zambezi River pushes enough water to fill an Olympic-sized swimming pool over the falls every two seconds. This produces a 1,300-ft- (400-m-) tall cloud of spray. In the dry season, the water level goes down, splitting the falls into four separate torrents.

Zigzagging river
The Zambezi River zigzags through six river gorges—four of which are shown here. These narrow, steep-sided valleys are carved as running water wears away the rock underneath. Victoria Falls lies at the top of the first of these gorges.

Haven for wildlife
This region of dry grasslands and bushes does not receive much rainfall, but there is enough spray from the falls for a tiny rain forest to thrive on the surrounding riverbanks. This provides a lush habitat for animals such as hippos, which are not found elsewhere in the area.

Devil's Pool
One of the ways to get a good view of Victoria Falls is from the top. Local guides take visitors to the Devil's Pool, a safe place right on the edge to sit and watch the water gushing past. The Devil's Pool is only accessible in the dry season, when the current is not too strong.

Rainbow forms as the Sun shines through the spray

Wall of rock keeps swimmers from falling over

Lascaux Cave paintings

Lascaux Cave is in the Dordogne region of southern France, an area famous for its caves.

In 1940, four teenage boys looking for treasure discovered the Lascaux Cave in France. Instead of gold and jewels, they found paintings, drawings, and engravings that covered the walls of the cave. These prehistoric pictures have been preserved for more than 16,000 years.

Axial gallery

Hall of Bulls

Nave

Passage

Apse

Shaft

Entrance

Silted-up chamber

Layout
The cave is located inside a limestone hill, with the entrance high up on a cliff. It is made up of several chambers—including the Shaft, the Apse, and the Hall of Bulls—that contain around 2,000 paintings and rock carvings.

Animal kingdom
Many of the cave paintings feature animals. This picture, known as "The Crossed Bison," is in the Nave. There are also paintings of extinct species, such as the cave hyena and woolly rhinoceros.

Hall of Bulls
The largest paintings are in the Hall of Bulls, which features giant bulls as well as stags and horses. The central bull is 11½ ft (3.5 m) long. The unidentified animal on the far left has been called a "unicorn" and is thought to represent a hunting spirit.

The wounded man
There is only one picture of a human in the entire cave. In it, a man appears to have been knocked over by the bull to his right. The little bird below is thought to represent his spirit.

Chamber of Felines

Needle

Harpoon

Saw

Tools of the trade
The Lascaux paintings were created during the last Ice Age. Because the Dordogne was not covered in ice at that time, the cave people were able to hunt caribou and make tools from bones and antlers.

Pigments used
The cave people used pigments made from crushed rocks and earth. The pigments were mixed with water and applied with a stick or a brush. They could also be dabbed on with cloth, sprayed with a hollow bone, or even spat out from the mouth.

Iron oxide was used as red color

Yellow ochre

Wall recreated using a 3-D survey of the real cave wall

Technician fitting together a re-creation of the cave paintings

Replica cave
The original cave has now been closed to protect the fragile paintings. Visitors can instead go to Lascaux II, a replica cave nearby.

35

Stonehenge

A circle of megaliths (giant stones), Stonehenge is one of the world's most famous Stone Age structures. Its most iconic feature is the trilithons—two large stones with a third laid across the top. This site may have been used for burials or rituals—but no one knows why and how it was built.

Stonehenge is located on the Salisbury Plain in southern England, UK.

Stone placed on top of two sarsen stones

Stages of construction

Stonehenge was built in stages, starting in around 3000 BCE. The site was originally a circular earthwork, and it is believed that a ring of wooden posts was then added. Later, these posts were replaced by a ring of smaller bluestones (blue-gray stones), followed by larger sarsen stones.

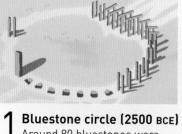

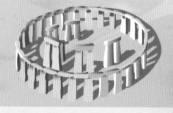

1 Bluestone circle (2500 BCE)
Around 80 bluestones were arranged in two circles. They were brought from Wales, around 200 miles (320 km) from the site.

2 Sarsen circle (2400 BCE)
The bluestones were replaced by a high circle of 30 sarsen stones. Inside the circle, five trilithons were placed in the shape of a horseshoe.

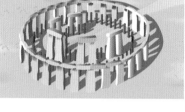

3 Full circle (2000 BCE)
The bluestones that had been removed earlier were put back as a circle and in the shape of a horseshoe within the sarsen stone circle.

Three-stone structure known as a trilithon

Huts made from woven stalks and mud

Settlement

The remains of a large settlement have been found at Durrington Walls, near Stonehenge. One theory is that these settlers created the stone structures as a burial site for their dead.

Carved lump would have been slotted into the hole of the slab above

Remains of outer circle of sarsen stones

Celtic legend

One of the theories is that the Druids—members of the priestly class of the Celts—built Stonehenge. However, studies show that the structure was completed long before the Celts came to England. Even so, modern Druids still hold ceremonies at the site twice a year.

Worn-away bluestone

Today's site

Stonehenge had around 165 stones when the circle was complete, but of these only 92 remain today. Many have either fallen or been worn away. A few of the standing stones have now been set in concrete to prevent them from falling.

Burial site

Graves found at Stonehenge have led to the theory that it was an ancient burial site for the people who built it. Several skeletons have been excavated in the area, and stone tools and weapons have been found in the graves.

Stone ax

Stone arrowheads

Stone axhead

Carhenge

Located in Nebraska, this replica of Stonehenge is made from old cars sprayed with gray paint. Jim Reinders built Carhenge as a memorial to his father, using a total of 38 cars.

Star gazing

Some theories suggest that Stonehenge was an astronomical observatory. This is based on the fact that the biggest stones line up with the sunrise and sunset at certain times of the year.

The Nasca Lines

Covered in hundreds of giant patterns, the Nasca Desert in Peru is the largest drawing board in the world. The Nasca Lines were created around 1,500 years ago, but lay forgotten until the late 1920s. Without an aircraft, it is impossible to see the designs in full.

The Nasca Lines are in southeastern Peru, about 12.5 miles (20 km) from the Pacific Ocean.

Geoglyphs

The Nasca Lines are geoglyphs—patterns on the ground made using rocks, gravel, soil, or even trees. Other examples of geoglyphs include the 2,000-year-old Paracas Candelabra in northern Peru and stone wheel patterns found in the Arabian Desert.

The Nasca Monkey, one of the many patterns seen on the Nasca Desert

Drawings on the ground

The Nasca people made the patterns by first clearing the dark upper rocks to uncover the paler soil underneath. They marked out the straight lines with rocks and scraped out the curves and spirals by hand.

Tail portion of the 305-ft- (93-m-) long Nasca Hummingbird

Monkey

Spider

Big pictures

The Nasca Lines cover an area of 100 sq miles (260 sq km). There are around 900 designs, all made between 400 and 650 CE. The largest patterns are almost 935 ft (385 m) long. Since this area receives little rain or wind, the lines have remained intact over the centuries.

Mysterious lines

Most of the Nasca Lines are spirals, geometric shapes, and straight lines. However, about 70 of them are pictures of animals and plants—including a monkey, a hummingbird, and this 154-ft- (47-m-) long spider. Adding to the mystery, some of these patterns are in the shape of animals not found in this region, such as the monkey.

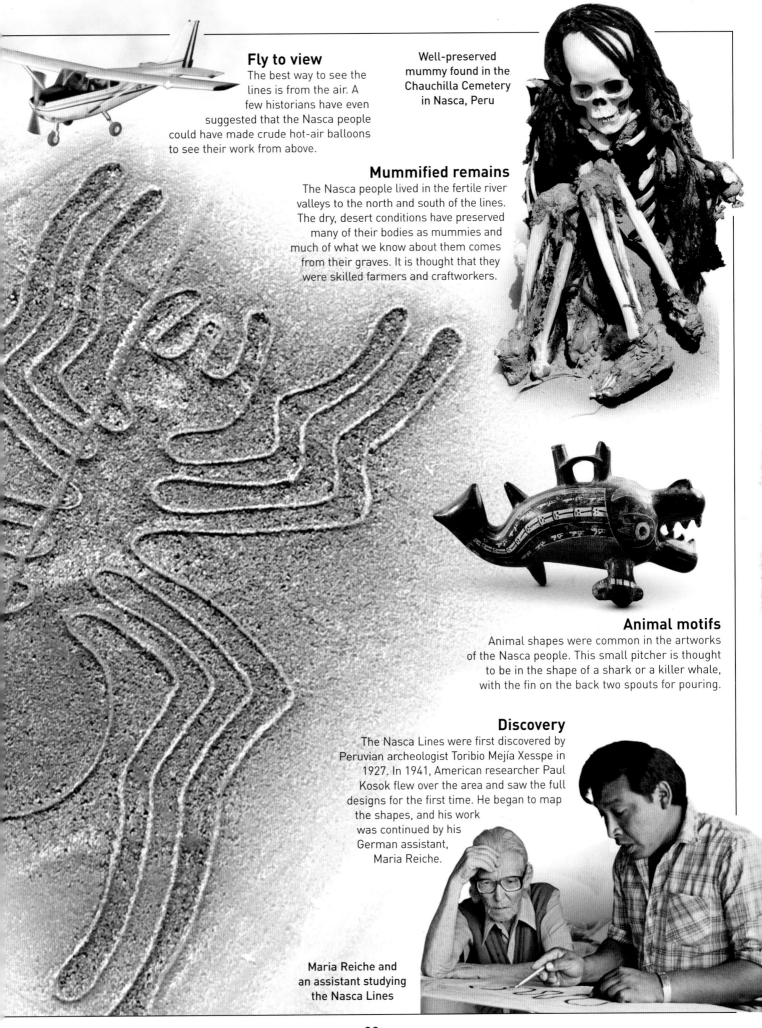

Fly to view

The best way to see the lines is from the air. A few historians have even suggested that the Nasca people could have made crude hot-air balloons to see their work from above.

Well-preserved mummy found in the Chauchilla Cemetery in Nasca, Peru

Mummified remains

The Nasca people lived in the fertile river valleys to the north and south of the lines. The dry, desert conditions have preserved many of their bodies as mummies and much of what we know about them comes from their graves. It is thought that they were skilled farmers and craftworkers.

Animal motifs

Animal shapes were common in the artworks of the Nasca people. This small pitcher is thought to be in the shape of a shark or a killer whale, with the fin on the back two spouts for pouring.

Discovery

The Nasca Lines were first discovered by Peruvian archeologist Toribio Mejía Xesspe in 1927. In 1941, American researcher Paul Kosok flew over the area and saw the full designs for the first time. He began to map the shapes, and his work was continued by his German assistant, Maria Reiche.

Maria Reiche and an assistant studying the Nasca Lines

Moai statues

Formed by three extinct volcanoes in the Pacific Ocean, Easter Island is home to nearly 900 enormous statues. Known as *moai*, these statues were placed along the island's coast around 1250–1500. All of them were built by the islanders as monuments to their ancestors. By the 19th century, many of the *moai* had been torn down, but no one is sure why.

Easter Island lies in the Pacific Ocean, 2,175 miles (3,500 km) from the coast of Chile.

Easter discovery
Although it had been inhabited since 700 CE, the island was only discovered by Europeans in 1722, when Dutch explorer Jacob Roggeveen landed on the coast. He named the island after the day of his arrival—Easter Sunday.

Pukao, *or topknot, is cut from a type of volcanic rock called red scoria*

Similar proportions
The *moai* were carved using rock from a volcanic crater. All of the statues have similar proportions; the huge head makes up a third of the statue. Each face has a wide chin, a long, pointed nose, and rectangular earlobes.

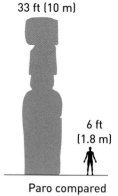

33 ft (10 m)

6 ft (1.8 m)

Paro compared to a human

Larger than life
Most *moai* are about 13 ft (4 m) high. The tallest, named Paro, is 33 ft (10 m) tall and weighs 90 tons (82 metric tons).

Ancient script

The islanders made carvings in a script known as Rongorongo. It contains hundreds of shapes, many resembling plants and animals. No one has been able to decipher it, but experts have suggested that the text is written from left to right, starting from the bottom left corner.

Rongorongo tablet carved on rosewood

Moving statues

The *moai*—weighing up to several tons—were carved at a quarry in the middle of the island and transported several miles to the coast. They may have been dragged on sleds or rocked from side to side to make them "walk."

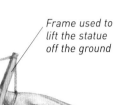

Frame used to lift the statue off the ground

Rope made from plant fibers

Birdman

Around 1500, the Rapa Nui began holding an annual race where young men from each clan would swim to a nearby island to collect tern eggs. The clan chief of the winner would became the "birdman" and would rule the island for a year.

Birdman, or *Tangata Manu*, carved into rock

The islanders

The people of Easter Island, known as the Rapa Nui, are Polynesian. Their language is similar to that spoken around Tahiti, another island more than 2,500 miles (4,000 km) away.

Cape made from softened bark fibers

Eye sockets held "eyes" made from carved white coral with a black obsidian "pupil"

Some statues have been buried up to their necks

Spirits of the ancestors

Each village on the island had several *moai* lined up together on a platform called *ahu*. The statues were thought to represent the spirits of important ancestors who watched over the village and protected the living.

Machu Picchu

An ancient stone city, now in ruins, Machu Picchu sits on a lush hillside in Peru. The name "Machu Picchu" means "old mountain," after the smaller of the two peaks that stand on each side of the city. Forgotten for almost 400 years, Machu Picchu was once inhabited by the Inca civilization.

Machu Picchu is located in the Andes Mountains in Peru, near the ancient city of Cusco.

Up in the clouds
Machu Picchu is set high up on a ridge in the middle of a tropical forest. Many people visit the site by train; others hike along the Inca Trail, a mountain path that used to connect the city to Cusco, the great Inca capital about 50 miles (80 km) away.

Central square

Empire builder
Machu Picchu was built for the Inca emperor Pachacuti around 1450. His kingdom stretched from modern-day Ecuador to Chile.

Steep cliffs on both sides of the city

Stone bricks fit closely together

Gold image of Inti

Earthquake-proof

Machu Picchu contains almost 200 buildings. To protect the structures from earthquakes, the Inca stonemasons used a special building technique. Instead of gluing the stones together using mortar, which cracks apart during quakes, they cut each stone to fit precisely into the one next to it.

Top of Huayna Picchu— the taller of the two peaks—was home to Inca priests

Artifact found at Machu Picchu

Sun worship

The Inca worshiped many gods, the most important of which was the Sun god, Inti, who was worshiped as the source of light and warmth, and as a protector of the people. Inti was especially important for the royal family because the Inca people believed that their emperors were direct descendants of the Sun god.

Royal retreat

Gold and silver treasures found at Machu Picchu suggest that the city was Pachacuti's country retreat. Because the city could not grow enough food for itself, its people must have brought in supplies along the Inca Trail.

Why was it abandoned?

Machu Picchu was abandoned around 1550. During this time, the Inca were at war with Spanish invaders and dying from diseases the Spanish had brought with them. Machu Picchu was not destroyed in this war; instead, its people appear to have simply left.

Painting showing a Spaniard attacking Inca warriors

Crops were grown on terraces cut into the side of the mountain

Rediscovery

Machu Picchu lay forgotten for centuries. In 1911, American explorer Hiram Bingham was taken to the area by a local boy. Bingham spent the next four years researching the amazing city.

The Acropolis

The Acropolis is in Athens, the capital city of Greece.

Built around 3,400 years ago, the Acropolis began as a citadel, or fortress, to provide a refuge from invaders. After being destroyed by the Persians, the Acropolis was rebuilt in the 5th century BCE. Its elegant new temples, including the Parthenon, celebrated the achievements of ancient Greece.

Theater mask from ancient Greece

View from the top

The Acropolis sits on a rocky hill 490 ft (150 m) above Athens. Around 20 buildings, now in ruins, remain today. Most of these were built between 450 and 430 BCE by Pericles, a great Athenian political leader.

The Parthenon, the largest building in the Acropolis, covered an area equal to eight tennis courts

Theater and drama

Music and drama were an important part of ancient Greek culture. The Theater of Dionysus, built into the cliff of the Acropolis, had room for an audience of 17,000 people.

The Erechtheion housed a sacred carving believed to have fallen from heaven

The Parthenon

Designed by the artist Phidias, the Parthenon is one of the finest remaining examples of ancient Greek architecture. Although the Parthenon is described as a temple, it was more like an art gallery filled with treasures. In 1687 CE, it was badly damaged by an explosion during a battle between Venice and Turkey.

Central hall, or cella, surrounded by solid walls

Carvings of mythical scenes above columns

Roof covered in marble tiles

There were 46 main marble columns

Gold-and-ivory statue of Athena in the main hall (removed by the Romans in the 5th century CE)

Wealthy Athenians came to admire the artworks inside

The Propylaea, the magnificent gateway to the Acropolis

Computer-generated cutaway model of the Parthenon as it stood in ancient Greece

Poseidon, the Greek god of the sea

Athena, the goddess of wisdom and justice

Athena

The Acropolis was built for Athena, the patron goddess of Athens. According to myth, she competed with the god Poseidon for the love of the city's people—and won.

Ancient Greek cameo, or carving, depicting the contest

Sporting contests

Every four years, Athens held the Panathenaic Games in a stadium near the Acropolis. Vases, such as this one, were filled with olive oil from a sacred grove dedicated to Athena and awarded as prizes.

Restoration

The Acropolis is being carefully reconstructed using marble cut from the original quarry. Since no one knows just how the buildings would have looked, the structures are held together with metal pins, which can be rearranged if new designs are discovered in the future.

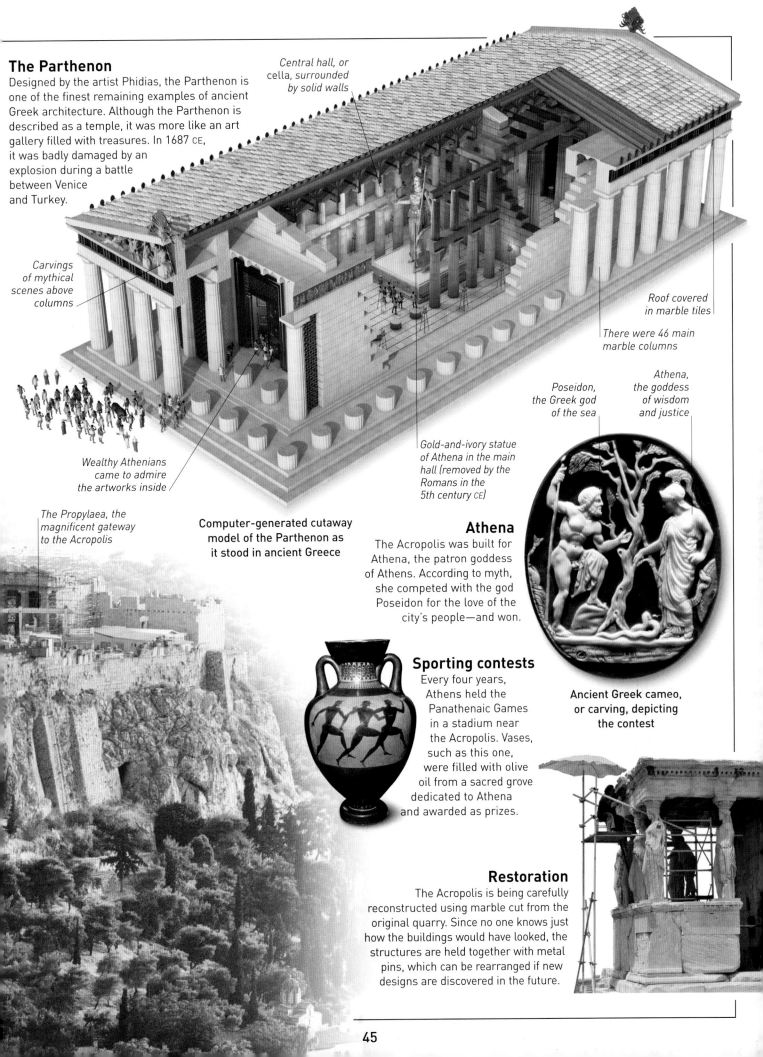

Petra

Petra is an ancient city in southern Jordan, halfway between the Dead Sea and the Red Sea.

Almost 2,000 years ago, Petra was a bustling desert city built by the Nabataeans, an ancient tribe of merchants. Today, all that remains is a site with massive structures carved into the mountainside. After 900 years as one of the world's wealthiest cities, Petra was badly damaged by earthquakes, and its people were forced to abandon it.

Discovery
In 1812, Swiss explorer Johann Ludwig Burckhardt became the first European to discover Petra after it was abandoned around 663 CE.

Sculpted in stone
The name "Petra" comes from the Greek word for "rock." The city's monuments are carved into the surrounding cliffs and the rooms inside it are hollowed-out caves. Petra is also called the "Rose city" because the sandstone rock-face into which it is built is pink and red in color.

The Monastery is as tall as a modern five-story building

Red sandstone cliffs

Caravan city

Merchants crossed the desert in caravans—convoys of camels laden with perfumes and spices. Petra was the crossing point of the routes between seaports and the cities of Damascus and Babylon (modern-day Iraq).

Cardamom came from India

Cinnamon came from Ethiopia

Frankincense came from Yemen

The mountain corridor

The main path leading to Petra is called the Siq, a narrow, winding, ¾-mile (1.2-km) gorge that cuts though the mountain. The Siq kept the city well-protected and very difficult to find. This explains why Petra remained undiscovered for many years.

Ornate pottery

It is thought that Petra was home to around 20,000 Nabataeans. Artifacts found in the city reveal that the people who lived here were highly skilled at making delicate plates and bowls for everyday use. Many items feature floral and geometric patterns.

Drinking bowl

Oil lamp

City of tombs

Nabataean tombs were built high up in the cliff and looked like grand houses from the outside. Inscriptions on some of the tombs provide details about people who were once buried here, some of whom were Nabataean kings.

Graves in a Petra tomb

Nabataean writing on clay tablet

Ancient script

The Nabataeans had their own alphabet, which gives us clues about where they came from. The writing was similar to Aramaic, the language spoken in this area around 2,000 years ago.

Sacred land

According to Hebrew scripture, Petra was built on the very spot where Moses, the leader of the Jews, struck a rock, bringing forth a stream of water and saving his people from thirst on their way to the Promised Land. Today, the valley is called Wadi Musa, which means "valley of Moses" in Arabic.

A 17th-century painting illustrating the story of Moses bringing water to his people

The Great Wall of China

The world's largest man-made structure, the Great Wall of China is more than 12,400 miles (20,000 km) long. Its construction began in the 2nd century BCE, with more extensions added over the next 1,700 years. The wall features watchtowers and gatehouses, forming a strong defense system.

The Great Wall runs through northern China, all the way to the East China Sea.

Desert fort

The fortresses on the Great Wall, known as passes, are the only places that travelers can cross over. The Jiayuguan fortress, situated in the Gobi Desert, protects the western end of the wall. Jiayuguan and the wall in this region are made from dried mud and stones.

The first emperor

Qin Shi Huangdi was the first emperor of China. Before his rule, China was split into many small countries, which often fought each other. Qin ended the wars in 221 BCE and ordered the wall to be built to mark the boundary of his empire.

The Ming wall

Most of the wall seen today was built during the reign of the Ming Dynasty, a family of emperors that ruled China from 1368 to 1644 CE. Much of this part of the wall is made from strong, durable brick.

Watchtowers, from where guards looked out for invaders

The Great Wall follows the top of the mountain ridge

Who was it keeping out?

The Great Wall was built as a defense against invaders. It could not, however, keep out the Mongol warlord Genghis Khan, who attacked the empire in the 13th century CE and conquered most of China.

Helpful dragon

Chinese folklore regards dragons as kindly creatures that live in rivers and mountains. According to legend, a helpful dragon laid out the course of the wall across the landscape.

Copper statue of a Chinese dragon

Into the sea

The Laolongtou is the easternmost fortress of the Great Wall where it meets the sea. It is also called the Old Dragon Head, because it looks like a stone dragon drinking water from the sea.

Marathon runners ascending a steep part of the wall

The wall today

Not all visitors to the Great Wall come to see the view. Every year, the wall hosts a marathon. Runners have to climb 5,164 steps during the race!

Steps on the wall can be very steep and uneven

The Eiffel Tower

The Eiffel Tower is one of the most recognizable structures in the world. Every year, more than 6 million tourists flock to the 1,063-ft (324-m) tall tower. On a clear day, visitors can see 37 miles (60 km) in every direction from the tower's upper level.

The Eiffel Tower is located on the south bank of the Seine River in Paris.

Radio transmissions

In 1903, a military radio station was set up at the top of the tower. It was later used to intercept enemy radio during World War I. Today, television and radio signals are broadcast from the tower.

The Eiffel Tower radio transmitter used in World War I

Third level is almost 900 ft (274 m) above the ground

Tokyo Tower

There are replicas of the Eiffel Tower all around the world. Opened in 1958 and 30 ft (9 m) taller than the Eiffel Tower, the Tokyo Tower in Japan is painted orange and white so that aircraft flying above can see it clearly.

Gustave Eiffel

The impressive tower design by Gustave Eiffel was chosen as the centerpiece for an international exhibition held in Paris in 1889. Eiffel had previously designed the interior supports of the Statue of Liberty in 1881.

Construction of the tower

It took 300 people more than two years to build the tower, which was completed in 1889. It is made of 18,038 steel components, held together with 2.5 million rivets. Each leg of the tower stands on its own supporting block, and the blocks are joined to each other by walls.

Higher portion is painted darker for a uniform effect

Second level was completed in 13 months

50

Philippe Petit about to complete his stunt

Balancing act

In 1989, Philippe Petit celebrated the tower's 100th birthday by walking along a 2,300-ft- (700-m-) long tightrope from the Palais de Chaillot museum complex to the second level of the Eiffel Tower.

Second level is 376 ft (115 m) above the ground

Towering the skyline

The Eiffel Tower was the tallest building in the world for 41 years, before New York's Chrysler Building was completed in 1930. It has viewing platforms for visitors on three levels, and restaurants on the first two.

First level is 187 ft (57 m) above the ground

To the top

Each level has a separate double-decker elevator to carry visitors. The Eiffel Tower has 1,710 steps in total, but visitors are only allowed to use the stairs up to the second level.

The pyramids of Giza

The three enormous pyramids of Giza are the burial site of three Egyptian rulers, or pharaohs. The tombs were built from millions of blocks of stone. The largest and oldest is the Great Pyramid. Its construction began around 2589 BCE, and at 482 ft (147 m) high, it held the record of the world's tallest building for more than 3,800 years.

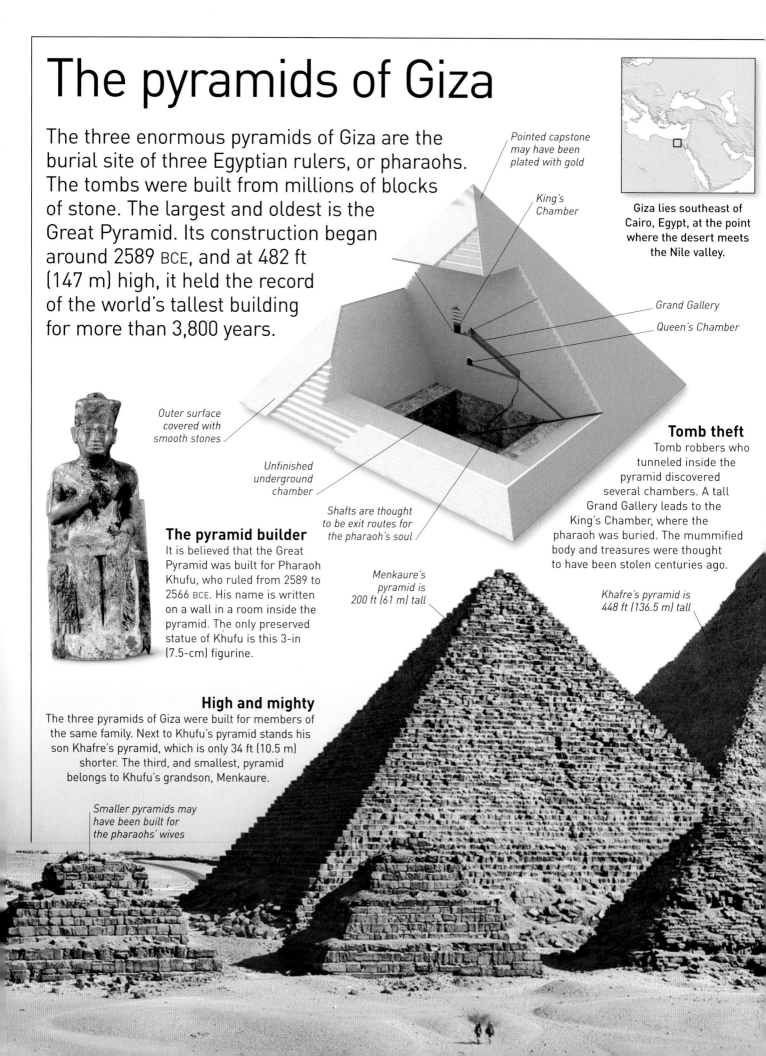

Pointed capstone may have been plated with gold

King's Chamber

Giza lies southeast of Cairo, Egypt, at the point where the desert meets the Nile valley.

Grand Gallery

Queen's Chamber

Outer surface covered with smooth stones

Unfinished underground chamber

Shafts are thought to be exit routes for the pharaoh's soul

Tomb theft

Tomb robbers who tunneled inside the pyramid discovered several chambers. A tall Grand Gallery leads to the King's Chamber, where the pharaoh was buried. The mummified body and treasures were thought to have been stolen centuries ago.

Menkaure's pyramid is 200 ft (61 m) tall

Khafre's pyramid is 448 ft (136.5 m) tall

The pyramid builder

It is believed that the Great Pyramid was built for Pharaoh Khufu, who ruled from 2589 to 2566 BCE. His name is written on a wall in a room inside the pyramid. The only preserved statue of Khufu is this 3-in (7.5-cm) figurine.

High and mighty

The three pyramids of Giza were built for members of the same family. Next to Khufu's pyramid stands his son Khafre's pyramid, which is only 34 ft (10.5 m) shorter. The third, and smallest, pyramid belongs to Khufu's grandson, Menkaure.

Smaller pyramids may have been built for the pharaohs' wives

Building the pyramid

It is thought that the pyramids were built by hauling stones up huge earthen ramps that ran around the outside. It would have taken tens of thousands of workers at least 10 years to complete one pyramid.

Model showing how ramps and ropes were used to move and lift stones

The Khufu ship is one of the world's oldest boats

Great Sphinx

Standing 1,700 ft (518 m) in front of Khafre's pyramid is the Great Sphinx, a statue of a creature with a lion's body and a human head. At 241 ft (73.5 m) long and 66.3 ft (20.2 m) high, it is the world's largest statue carved from a single piece of stone.

The Great Sphinx guards the route to the pyramids

Khufu ship

In 1954, 1,224 wooden parts were found buried at the foot of the Great Pyramid. They were assembled into a 143-ft (43.6-m) boat known as the Khufu ship. Ancient Egyptians believed that Pharaoh Khufu would use it to sail through the heavens with the Sun god Ra.

Smooth limestone covering the top section still remains

The Great Pyramid is made of 2.6 million limestone blocks

Robot explorers

Archeologists use small robots to explore the mysterious shafts that run through the pyramids. The Djedi robot has a flexible camera that can look around corners, a drill for digging through blockages, and an ultrasound scanner that can detect hollow spaces.

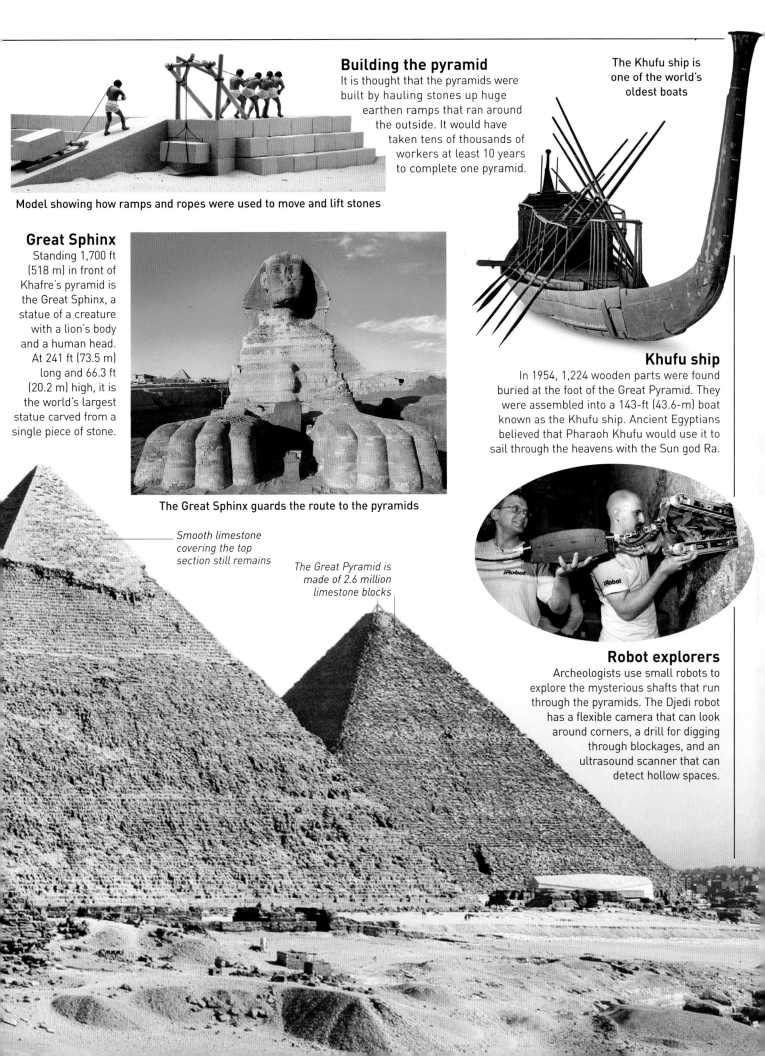

The Colosseum

In the heart of the busy city of Rome, Italy, stands a 2,000-year-old round building, towering over its modern surroundings. The Colosseum—the world's largest amphitheater—was built as an entertainment venue for the Romans. This massive arena once hosted epic stage shows and blood-thirsty gladiator battles.

The Colosseum is in Rome, the capital of Italy.

Brick supports added in the 1800s to strengthen the old wall

Grand venture

The construction of the Colosseum began in 72 CE during the reign of Emperor Vespasian, the first Roman ruler from the Flavian family. The theater was completed under the rule of Vespasian's son, Titus, in 80 CE.

The structure

The Colosseum's walls were built from bricks covered in fine, white limestone. Much of the 157 ft (48 m) outer wall has collapsed over the years, mainly due to earthquakes. Most of the walls seen today were originally on the inside of the structure.

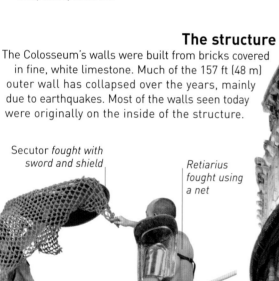

Secutor fought with sword and shield

Retiarius fought using a net

Gladiator games

The gladiators who fought in the Colosseum were highly trained slaves who fought one-on-one or in teams. The emperor and crowd would decide if the winning gladiator should kill the loser or spare him to fight another day.

Inside the arena

An amphitheater is a circular, open-air arena surrounded by seats. The Colosseum could hold up to 87,000 people in three tiers. The hypogeum, a system of tunnels, ran beneath the amphitheater and was used to transport gladiators, performers, and animals to the arena.

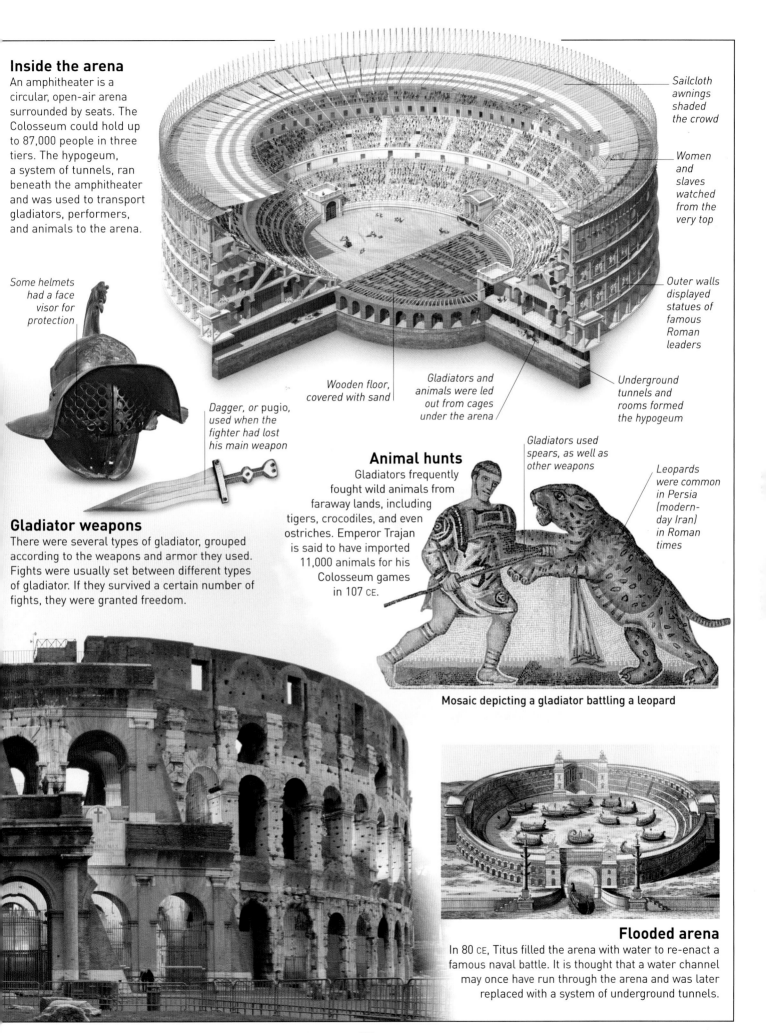

Sailcloth awnings shaded the crowd

Women and slaves watched from the very top

Outer walls displayed statues of famous Roman leaders

Some helmets had a face visor for protection

Dagger, or pugio, used when the fighter had lost his main weapon

Wooden floor, covered with sand

Gladiators and animals were led out from cages under the arena

Underground tunnels and rooms formed the hypogeum

Gladiators used spears, as well as other weapons

Leopards were common in Persia (modern-day Iran) in Roman times

Gladiator weapons

There were several types of gladiator, grouped according to the weapons and armor they used. Fights were usually set between different types of gladiator. If they survived a certain number of fights, they were granted freedom.

Animal hunts

Gladiators frequently fought wild animals from faraway lands, including tigers, crocodiles, and even ostriches. Emperor Trajan is said to have imported 11,000 animals for his Colosseum games in 107 CE.

Mosaic depicting a gladiator battling a leopard

Flooded arena

In 80 CE, Titus filled the arena with water to re-enact a famous naval battle. It is thought that a water channel may once have run through the arena and was later replaced with a system of underground tunnels.

Angkor Wat

The largest religious monument in the world, Angkor Wat was constructed during the reign of King Suryavarman II in the early 12th century. In Khmer, the language of Cambodia, "Angkor Wat" means "temple city."

Angkor Wat is located in northern Cambodia, near the city of Siem Reap.

Statue of Vishnu with eight arms

Place of worship
Khmer kings, especially Suryavarman II, were devout worshipers of Vishnu, the supreme god in Hinduism. A shrine dedicated to Vishnu is located in the upper gallery of Angkor Wat's central tower.

Stone carvings
Angkor Wat's main building is enclosed by three concentric galleries. The inner walls of these galleries are covered in friezes (stone carvings) depicting stories of Hindu gods and heroes. The frieze called "Churning of the Sea of Milk" measures more than 2,625 ft (800 m). It is said to be the longest frieze in the world.

Home of the gods
Angkor Wat was built in the shape of a lotus flower, an important symbol in Hinduism. The central tower represents the five-peaked Mount Meru, a mythical mountain believed to be the home of Lord Brahma, the Hindu god of creation.

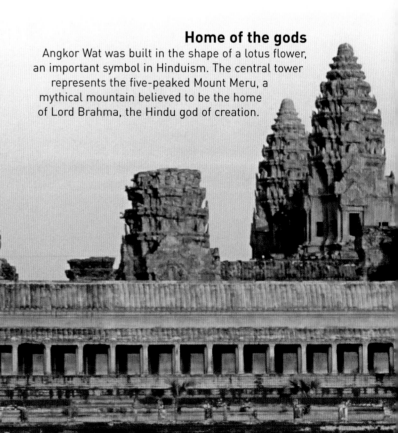

Aligned with the Sun

Angkor Wat lines up with the points of the compass, with the main entrance pointing west. During the spring and fall equinox (the two days of the year when day and night are exactly the same length) the Sun rises directly behind the central tower.

National symbol

An image of Angkor Wat appears in the center of the Cambodian flag. This magnificent temple has become a national symbol of Cambodia's ancient Khmer heritage.

Rooted to the ground

The region around Angkor Wat contains many ancient temples and palaces. Many were abandoned, and the surrounding jungle grew around them—or, in the case of the Ta Prohm temple, on top of them.

Buddhism

About 50 years after Angkor Wat was completed, the Khmer converted to Buddhism, which had become popular during the reign of Jayavarman VII. Angkor Wat became a Buddhist temple and remains one today, except for a brief period in the 13th century when it was converted back to a Hindu temple.

Central tower,
213 ft (65 m) high

The Taj Mahal

Built in the 17th century, the Taj Mahal (meaning "crown of palaces") is a beautiful example of Mogul architecture—a mix of Indian, Islamic, and Persian styles. This white marble tomb is cube-shaped and looks the same from all sides. It is reflected in a long pool set in the center of the beautiful gardens.

The Taj Mahal is located beside the Yamuna River in Agra, in northern India.

Red petals made with carnelian stones

Art and decoration
The decorations inside the tomb are made from polished gemstones set into marble. The lattice windows are composed of sheets of marble with ornate holes cut into them.

Arabic words are written in black marble

Writing on the wall
The Arabic writing on the walls of the Taj Mahal is taken from the Qur'an, the holy book of Islam. The words were written first on paper, then traced onto the stone before being chiseled out and filled with black marble.

Each corner has an identical 134½-ft (41-m) minaret, or tower

Shah Jahan and Mumtaz Mahal

The Mogul emperor Shah Jahan built the Taj Mahal in memory of his wife Mumtaz Mahal, who died in 1631. He used only white marble because white (not black) is the color of mourning in Islamic tradition.

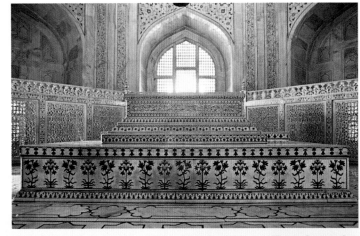

Royal tombs

In the ornate main chamber, two cenotaphs, or empty tombs, provide a memorial to Shah Jahan and his wife. Their actual graves lie in an undecorated underground vault, or burial chamber, that is closed to the public.

Each minaret of the tomb has the same chhatri, *or canopy, design*

Height of the dome matches the building's width

Pishtaq, *or archway*

Plinth, *or marble base*

Persian influences

The design of the Taj Mahal was greatly influenced by that of the tomb of Humayun—Shah Jahan's great-grandfather and the second Mogul emperor. Built in Delhi in 1570, the red sandstone structure was the first example of a garden tomb—a Persian-style building that used symmetry.

Neuschwanstein Castle

With its ornate spires and tall towers, Neuschwanstein Castle looks like something out of a fairy tale. This lavish palace was built in the late 19th century as a luxury country retreat for Ludwig II, King of Bavaria. Designed to look like a medieval castle, it took about 18 years to build.

Neuschwanstein Castle is located in the far southwest of Germany, in the foothills of the Alps.

King Ludwig II

The "mad" monarch

Ludwig II invested in many grand projects and eventually ran out of money. His ministers wanted to replace him and had him declared insane. On June 12, 1886, Ludwig II was imprisoned, and the following day, he was found dead in a lake. It is thought that he may have been killed while trying to escape.

Glass painting

Although the castle was constructed using modern building techniques, it was decorated in a traditional style. The stained-glass windows in the king's bedroom depict his family's coats of arms. The blue-and-white checks are the symbol of Bavaria.

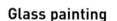

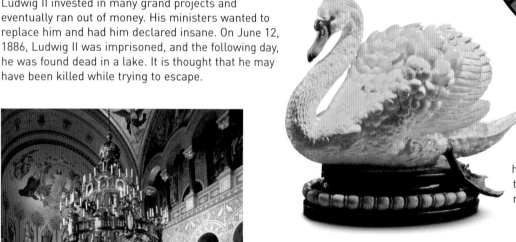

Swan King

Also known as the Swan King, Ludwig II modeled himself on the myth of Lohengrin—a knight who rescued a damsel in distress on a boat pulled by a swan. The king filled his castle with decorations based on the swan. The castle's name, in fact, means "new swan stone."

Paying tribute

Neuschwanstein Castle appears on the back of Germany's €2 coin. On completion in 1886, the castle was turned into a tourist attraction in an attempt to pay off its huge building costs.

Room at the top

Built at the very top of the castle, the Throne Hall is one of only 15 rooms in the castle that were fully completed—the rest were never beautified. However, a throne was never installed in the room.

Painting in the castle

Fairy-tale castle
With its soaring towers and grand staircases, Neuschwanstein Castle has become the inspiration for castles in many modern depictions of fairy tales. The Sleeping Beauty Castle, which opened in 1955 in Disneyland, California, was modeled on Neuschwanstein Castle.

Main tower rises 213 ft (65 m) high

Statue of knight with shield and lance

Painting of St. George slaying a dragon

Rectangular tower above guardhouse

Myths and legends
Ludwig II was a great friend of the composer Richard Wagner, whose operas were based on European myths and medieval romances. Murals that depict scenes from these stories can be seen on the castle walls. The painting above shows the warrior Siegfried slaying a dragon named Fafner.

Ludwig II lived in the gatehouse during the castle's construction

Burj Khalifa

At 2,717 ft (828 m), the Burj Khalifa is the world's tallest building. It took 7,500 workers six years to complete construction. Almost 120,000 tons (110,000 metric tons) of concrete—the weight of 100,000 elephants—and 43,000 tons (39,000 metric tons) of steel bars were used to build this tower.

The Burj Khalifa is in Dubai in the United Arab Emirates (UAE).

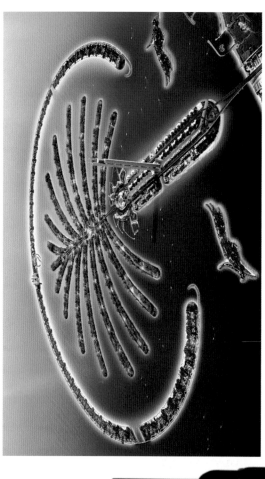

A computer-generated model of the man-made island Palm Jumeirah

Palm Islands

The Palm Islands are two artificial islands, each shaped like a palm tree. The coastline of one of the islands, the Palm Jumeirah, is 49 miles (78 km) long! Visitors can see these islands from the Burj's observation deck on the 124th floor, which also offers views of the Persian Gulf and the Arabian Desert.

Special glass keeps out the desert heat

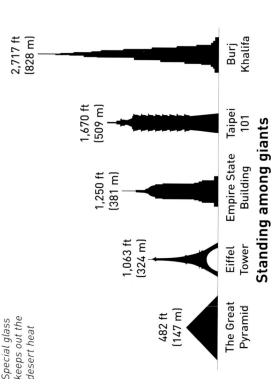

482 ft (147 m)	1,063 ft (324 m)	1,250 ft (381 m)	1,670 ft (509 m)	2,717 ft (828 m)
The Great Pyramid	Eiffel Tower	Empire State Building	Taipei 101	Burj Khalifa

Standing among giants

In 2010, the Burj Khalifa replaced the Taipei 101 tower in Taiwan as the world's tallest building. The last building in the Middle East to hold this record was the Great Pyramid in Egypt (see pp.52–53), which held the title for more than 3,800 years.

Reaching new heights

The Burj Khalifa has 163 floors, housing 1,000 apartments, offices, and hotels. Although its elevator ride distance is the longest in the world, it takes only a minute to reach the top. The tower also features the world's highest restaurant (on the 122nd floor) and the highest swimming pool (on the 76th floor).

Wings narrow in 27 steps

Central part of the building rises upward

Top-down view

Desert flower

The design of the Burj Khalifa was inspired by the spider lily, a desert flower. The tower's three wings are based on the flower's petals. The wings get narrower with height, which makes the building very strong.

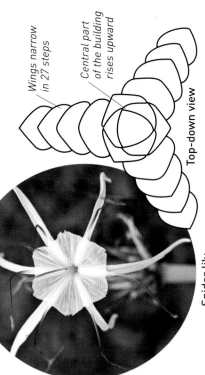

Spider lily

Performing fountain

The Dubai Fountain, the largest "performing" water display in the world, is set in the artificial lake around the tower. It sprays 22,000 gallons (83,000 liters) of water 500 ft (150 m) in the air.

Window cleaning

Most of the tower's 24,348 windows are washed by automated machines. However, from floor 109 upward, they are cleaned by hand by a team of 36 specially trained window washers.

Window washer hangs from special ropes

Lower section houses a hotel

Scaling the heights

Daring climber Alain Robert took just 6 hours to scale the Burj Khalifa using only a rope and safety harness. In 2010, Nasr Al Niyadi and Omar Al Hegelan used a crane on the 160th floor to make the world's highest parachute jump from a building.

Fireworks

The Burj Khalifa opened with a bang on January 4, 2010. The ceremony featured 10,000 fireworks and a laser light show. This was outdone on New Year's Eve 2013 by a 6-minute display using more than 500,000 fireworks—the world's largest-ever fireworks display.

63

Ancient wonders

Ancient Greek travelers were the first people to create a list of the world's most amazing man-made structures—known today as the Seven Wonders of the Ancient World. Only one of these—the pyramids of Giza—still remains, while historical records tell us what the rest might have looked like.

KEY

📍 The ancient wonders are all near the Mediterranean Sea

Temple of Artemis

Built in 550 BCE near Ephesus on the coast of modern-day Turkey, the Temple of Artemis was dedicated to Artemis, the Greek goddess of hunting. It was rebuilt three times before it was finally destroyed in 268 CE by a fierce and powerful tribe called the Goths.

Third version of the temple had more than 127 columns

Statue of Zeus

Temple of Artemis

Colossus of Rhodes

Mausoleum at Halicarnassus

Hanging Gardens of Babylon

Mediterranean Sea

Pharos of Alexandria

The pyramids of Giza

Where in the world

Most of the wonders were built in Greek cities around 2,000–2,500 years ago. However, the list also includes wonders from older civilizations, such as ancient Egypt and Babylon (in modern-day Iraq).

The pyramids of Giza

The pyramids of Giza, in Egypt, were already ancient—around 2,000 years old—by the time Greek travelers wrote about them. Much of what we know of the pyramids comes from the writings of the ancient Greek historian Herodotus, who visited the tombs in the 5th century BCE.

Pharos of Alexandria

The world's largest lighthouse in ancient times, the Pharos of Alexandria was built in the 3rd century BCE and stood around 425 ft (130 m) high. It guided ships into the port of Alexandria, an Egyptian city founded by the Greek conqueror Alexander the Great. The building gradually collapsed after being damaged in three earthquakes, in 956 CE, 1303 CE, and 1323 CE.

Ships could sail safely by the light of the Pharos

Hanging Gardens of Babylon

According to legend, King Nebuchadnezzar II of Babylon created the Hanging Gardens for his wife in around 600 BCE. The gardens had many levels, with exotic plants hanging from stepped terraces. Experts disagree about what the gardens looked like and whether they even existed!

Channels brought water from the Euphrates River

Gardens built on a brick pyramid

Colossus of Rhodes

This marble statue is a replica of the original brass version that once stood in the ancient Greek city of Rhodes. Built in 292 BCE, the 147-ft (45-m) statue fell during an earthquake around 56 years later.

The head is said to be modeled on that of Alexander the Great

Statue of Zeus

This statue of Zeus (king of the Greek gods) was built by the Greek artist Phidias. It was erected in around 435 BCE in Olympia, the location of the ancient Olympic Games. The statue was destroyed about 800 years later, but no one knows exactly how it happened.

Throne decorated with ivory, gold, and precious stones

Mausoleum at Halicarnassus

In 350 BCE, Mausolus, the governor of southwestern Turkey, built himself a giant 131-ft- (40-m-) tall tomb in the city of Halicarnassus (modern-day Bodrum, Turkey). The tomb became known as the Mausoleum. Its four outer walls feature carvings of battle scenes, as well as statues of gods and goddesses.

Record breakers

Various natural processes have combined to create some of the most spectacular scenery in the world—from giant caves and high mountains, to tall geysers and deep trenches—which are often formed over millions of years. Today, people from all over the globe travel great distances to visit these record-breaking natural wonders.

Longest river

Name: Nile River

Location: Africa

Length: 4,258 miles (6,853 km)

The Nile is the world's longest river, stretching north from East Africa to the Mediterranean. It flows through 10 countries in Africa, although most of it lies within Egypt and Sudan.

Tallest mountain

Name: Mauna Kea

Location: Hawaii

Height: 13,803 ft (4,207 m)

Mauna Kea is the world's tallest mountain from base to peak. Much of the volcano is under the sea, and so it does not rise as high above the ground as Mount Everest (see pp.6–7).

Deepest trench

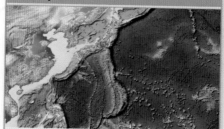

Name: Mariana Trench

Location: Western Pacific Ocean

Maximum depth: 6.7 miles (10.9 km)

The Mariana Trench is the deepest place in the world. If Mount Everest were set inside it, there would still be around 1.2 miles (2 km) of water left above its peak.

Most active volcano

Name: Mount Kīlauea

Location: Hawaii

Last eruption: January 3, 1983–Present

Mount Kīlauea is the world's most active volcano. Its current eruption began in 1983 and still continues today, making this eruption the longest ever recorded in the world.

Largest ocean

Name: Pacific Ocean

Location: From the Arctic to Antarctica

Area: 63,784,076 sq miles (165,200,000 sq km)

Covering almost one-third of Earth's surface, the Pacific is the world's largest ocean. It is twice the size of the Atlantic, the second largest ocean.

Largest cave

Name: Són Đoòng Cave

Location: Vietnam

Maximum height: 650 ft (200 m)

Són Đoòng, the world's largest cave, is 5.6 miles (9 km) long and 492 ft (150 m) wide. The roof has collapsed in some places, letting in sunlight and allowing plants to grow inside the cave.

Largest forest

Name: Amazon Rain Forest

Location: South America

Area: 2.3 million sq miles (6 million sq km)

The largest forest in the world, the Amazon has more than 12,000 species of trees. More than half of the Earth's plant and animal species live in the Amazon Rain Forest.

Largest grassland

Name: Eurasian steppe

Location: From Hungary to China

Length: Around 5,000 miles (8,000 km)

A vast plain running through Europe and Asia, the Eurasian steppe is the world's largest grassland. It is too dry for a forest to grow, but it gets enough rain for grasses and shrubs to thrive.

Largest ice shelf

Name: Ross Ice Shelf

Location: Ross Sea, Antarctica

Area: 188,000 sq miles (487,000 sq km)

An ice shelf is a frozen sheet of freshwater, reaching from the coast into the ocean. The Ross Ice Shelf is the largest in the world (by area) and is 2,000–10,000 ft (600–3,000 m) thick.

Tallest active geyser

Name: Steamboat Geyser

Location: Yellowstone National Park

Eruption height: 375–425 ft (115–130 m)

The Steamboat Geyser is the world's tallest geyser, reaching twice the height of Old Faithful (see pp.12–13). On eruption, it completely drains the underground Cistern Spring nearby.

Largest island

Name: Greenland

Location: Between Arctic and Atlantic Ocean

Area: 836,330 sq miles (2,166,086 sq km)

Greenland is the world's largest island. A third of it is covered in ice, which can be up to 1.8 miles (3 km) thick. If all the ice melted, the oceans would rise by 23 ft (7 m).

Largest desert

Name: Antarctic Desert

Location: Antarctica

Area: 5,339,573 sq miles (13,829,430 sq km)

A desert is a hot or cold area with little or no fresh liquid water. While the Sahara is the largest hot desert, Antarctica (made of solid ice) is the largest desert of all.

Highest tides

Name: Bay of Fundy

Location: Canada

Height of tides: Up to 53.5 ft (16.3 m)

The Bay of Fundy is in the Gulf of Maine in Canada. At high tide, this funnel-shaped gulf pushes rising water into the small bay, creating the world's highest tides.

Largest lake

Name: Lake Superior

Location: North America

Area: 31,820 sq miles (82,414 sq km)

The largest lake in the world (by area), Lake Superior is 350 miles (563 km) long and 160 miles (257 km) wide. The lake is famous for its crystal-clear water.

Highest waterfall

Name: Angel Falls

Location: Venezuela, South America

Height: 3,212 ft (979 m)

The Angel Falls is the highest uninterrupted waterfall in the world. It is 15 times higher than the famous Niagara Falls, which straddles Canada and the United States.

Longest fjord

Name: Scoresby Sund

Location: Greenland

Area: 14,700 sq miles (38,000 sq km)

A fjord is a long, narrow stretch of water surrounded by steep cliffs. Scoresby Sund, in the Greenland Sea, is the largest and longest system of fjords in the world.

Man-made wonders

Today's man-made wonders include huge skyscrapers of steel and glass, or vast tunnels, roads, and bridges that transform the landscape. These man-made wonders show us how technological skills have evolved over the centuries.

Tallest skyscrapers

Although the US was the first country to build skyscrapers in the 1880s, Asia is home to the world's tallest buildings today. Plans to build towers more than 3,300 ft (1,000 m) tall are currently underway.

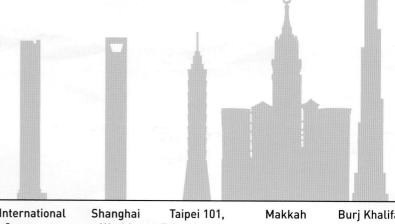

| International Commerce Center, China 1,588 ft (484 m) | Shanghai World Financial Center, China 1,614 ft (492 m) | Taipei 101, Taiwan, China 1,671 ft (509 m) | Makkah Royal Clock Tower Hotel, Saudi Arabia 1,971 ft (601 m) | Burj Khalifa, Dubai 2,717 ft (828 m) |

Wonders in danger

Although most ancient buildings are protected by heritage organizations, many are still in danger of destruction. In the past, treasures were often stolen from these sites, or taken to be reused in other buildings. Today, sites need protection from damage caused by visitors, natural processes, and modern development.

Most visited man-made wonders

Every year millions of tourists flock to see the wonders of the world. The eight most popular man-made wonders alone are visited by more than 70 million people every year.

Famous sites

 Mount Wutai, China 3,302,000

Ephesus, Turkey 3,500,000

The pyramids of Giza, Egypt 4,000,000

Teotihuacán, Mexico 4,200,000

Golden Temple, India 5,500,000

Imperial Palaces of the Ming and Qing Dynasties, China 7,000,000

Mausoleum of the First Qin Emperor, China 18,000,000

The Great Wall of China, China 24,200,000

0 5 10 15 20 25
Number of people who visited these sites in 2009

Abu Mena Ruins, Egypt
Built in the 4th century CE, Abu Mena was a center for Christian pilgrims. Today, its ruins are in danger of being washed away by water channeled into the area for farming.

El Mirador, Guatemala
Discovered in 1926 in the thick jungles of Central America, this huge Mayan city dates back 2,500 years. The ancient city has been exposed to many threats, such as logging, looting, and road building.

Iconic statues of the world

Statues are built for many reasons—to celebrate the life of a person or an event, as art, or for worship. Shown here are some of the giant statues around the world as they stand today.

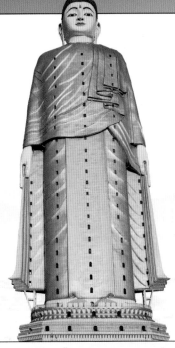

Christ the Redeemer, Brazil
125 ft (38 m)

The Motherland Calls, Russia
285 ft (87 m)

Statue of Liberty, USA
305 ft (93 m)

Laykyun Setkyar Buddha, Myanmar 381 ft (116 m)

Chersonesus, Ukraine
The ancient Greeks set up a colony at Chersonesus in Crimea (modern-day Ukraine) 2,500 years ago. Today, the ruins are being torn down to make way for housing.

Bam, Iran
Built 2,600 years ago, the ancient fortress of Bam is the world's largest mud building. In 2003, it was badly damaged in an earthquake.

Old City of Jerusalem, Jerusalem
Built around the holy sites of Islam, Judaism, and Christianity, the city has been fought over by different religious communities for centuries. The ongoing conflict still threatens the Old City.

Kasubi Tombs, Uganda
The kings of the Buganda people—Uganda's largest ethnic group—are buried in thatched tombs, parts of which mysteriously burned down in 2010.

Engineering marvels
Roads, railroads, bridges, tunnels, and airports may often seem unremarkable. However, even the most ordinary-looking structures involve precision engineering. This makes the record-breaking examples all the more amazing.

Longest road
The Pan-American Highway in the US spans 30,000 miles (48,000 km).

Longest railroad
Russia's Trans-Siberian Railroad is the longest continuous railroad at 5,753 miles (9,259 km).

Largest airport
Saudi Arabia's King Fahd International Airport covers 301 sq miles (780 sq km).

Longest railroad tunnel
The Seikan Tunnel in Japan stretches 33.5 miles (53.8 km).

Longest bridge
The Danyang–Kunshan Bridge, China, measures 102.4 miles (164.8 km).

Longest road tunnel
The Lærdal Tunnel runs 15 miles (24.5 km) under Norway's mountains.

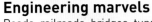

Glossary

ABORIGINES
The people who are native to Australia and have lived there since before the European settlers arrived.

AHU
The platform on which the Easter Island statues, or *moai*, were erected.

AMPHITHEATER
An open-air theater, usually with the seats arranged in a circle or oval around a central arena.

ARTIFACT
An object made by a human being, often of historical or cultural importance.

BACTERIA
Microscopic organisms found in water, soil, air, and in and on plants and animals.

BAY
An inlet of a sea or a lake that curves in toward land.

CANYON
A deep valley formed when a river cuts through a mountain.

CAVERN
A large cave. Caves form naturally due to rock erosion caused by water seeping through the ground. Caves can extend deep underground.

CENOTAPH
An empty tomb used as a monument to someone whose remains are buried elsewhere.

CITADEL
A fortress, usually on a hill, protecting a city.

CIVILIZATION
An organized society in a particular area with a set way of life, culture, and language.

COLUMN
A pillar that is used to hold up a roof, arch, or other parts of structures.

Olivine crystal

CORAL
A marine animal, with stony skeletons, that can form colonies. These skeletons can build up to form coral reefs.

CRATER
A large, bowl-shaped depression in the ground, usually caused by a volcanic eruption or the impact of a meteorite.

CRYSTAL
A gemlike mineral with a regular pattern that forms naturally. The process by which a crystal is formed is called crystallization.

FJORD
A deep valley created by a glacier now flooded by the sea.

FORTRESS
A heavily protected building, usually defended by an army.

FOSSIL
The remains or impression of a living thing, usually preserved in rock.

FRONTIER
A border separating two political regions.

GEODE
A mass of crystals that forms inside a space in a rock.

GEOGLYPH
A pattern made on the ground using rocks, stones, trees, and soil.

GEYSER
A natural spring that sprays boiling water and steam from the ground into the air.

GLADIATOR
A person in ancient Rome trained to fight against other people or wild animals in an arena in front of an audience.

GORGE
A deep, narrow valley, usually with steep cliffs on each side.

GRASSLANDS
A large, open area covered in grass, with few trees.

HOMINID
The group of animals that includes humans, along with chimpanzees and gorillas.

A lattice screen at the Taj Mahal, India

HYPOGEUM
An underground complex, which usually has tunnels, dungeons, and chambers.

LATTICE
An ornamental, netlike framework used to decorate buildings.

LAVA
Molten rock that has erupted onto the surface from deep within Earth's crust.

Model showing life in ancient Egyptian civilization

MAGMA
Molten rock formed deep within the Earth.

MARINE RESERVE
An area of the ocean where fish and other sea animals are protected.

MICROSCOPIC
An object that is so small that it can only be seen through a microscope.

MIGRATION
A journey, usually along a set route, in search of food and water. Animals migrate in response to changes in season.

MINARET
A slender tower, usually part of a mosque (an Islamic place of worship), with a narrow balcony.

MINERAL
A naturally occurring, solid substance that is inorganic (not made from the remains of plants and animals). Minerals cement together to form rocks.

MONASTERY
A place where members of a religious community live and practice their religion.

MUMMY
A body of a human or animal that has been preserved from decay.

MYTH
An old, traditional story usually about how natural phenomena or social customs came to exist.

NOMAD
A person without a permanent home who moves regularly.

OASIS
An area in a desert where water is found.

OUTBACK
The remote and usually uninhabited inland regions of Australia.

PHARAOH
The title given to the rulers of ancient Egypt.

PLATEAU
A wide, flat area of high land that rises above its surroundings.

POLYP
An individual organism, part of a coral colony.

PREDATOR
An animal that feeds by catching and eating other animals, which are called prey.

The spider is a predator of the ladybug

QUARRY
A place from which stone, rock, slate, or other material is removed for use in building.

REEF
A part of the seabed, often near land, and close to the surface of the water. It can be made of rock, or built up over centuries by corals that have hard stony skeletons.

Coral reef in Indonesia

RIDGE
A long, narrow hilltop or mountain range. It also refers to the top edge of a canyon.

SAFARI
A journey taken to watch wild animals in their natural habitat.

SALT FLAT
A large area of flat land, covered in a layer of salt.

SANDSTONE
A rock made from ancient sand grains.

SAVANNA
A dry grassland, where there is too little rainfall for forests to grow. Instead, fast-growing grasses cover the ground.

SHINTO
A religion that originated in Japan, based on the worship of nature and one's ancestors.

SINKHOLES
Holes that appear suddenly after rock and earth is washed away by water and the ground collapses in on itself.

SPRING
A place where underground water flows to the surface.

STEPPE
A vast, flat area of land with few trees, especially in eastern Europe and Asia.

STRATOVOLCANO
A cone-shaped volcano with steep slopes and made of many layers of lava and ash.

TENTACLE
A flexible, armlike limb of some animals that is used for grasping, moving, or sensing.

TEPUI
A native word that refers to a type of flat-topped mountain found in South America.

TRENCH
A deep, narrow ditch in the ground, often caused by movement of the Earth's crust.

VOLCANO
An opening in the Earth's crust through which magma, ash, and hot gases erupt; the structure created by the eruption is also called a volcano.

WATERING HOLE
A pool in the ground from which animals regularly drink.

WETLAND
An area of land covered with shallow water for large parts of the year. Lagoons, swamps, and marshes are all wetlands.

WOODLAND
An area covered by trees.

Index

Acknowledgments

Dorling Kindersley would like to thank: Hazel Beynon for text editing; Helen Peters for the index; Stewart Wild for proofreading; Esha Banerjee and Sonam Mathur for editorial assistance; and Anis Sayyed and Govind Mittal for design assistance.

The publishers would also like to thank the following for their kind permission to reproduce their photographs:
(Key: a-above; b-below/bottom; c-center; f-far; l-left; r-right; t-top)

1 Corbis: 145 (c). 2 Alamy Images: Sabena Jane Blackbird (cb). Dorling Kindersley: Hopi Learning Center, Arizona (tr). Dreamstime.com: Engin Korkmaz (l); Neophuket (br). Getty Images: Lane Oatey / Blue Jean Images (t); Siede Preis / Photodisc (tl). Robert Harding Picture Library: Gonzalo Azumendi (c). 3 Alamy Images: McPHOTO / vario images (tr). 123RF.com: Raweewat Tuntisavee (tl). Alamy Images: Deco (cl). Dreamstime.com: Luciano Mortula (br). Getty Images: Stephane De Sakutin / AFP (bl). 5 Dreamstime.com: Zhukovsky (br). 6 Press Association Images: AP (cra). SuperStock: imagebroker.net (r). 7 Corbis: Stringer / Nepal / Reuters (cr). Dreamstime.com: Dmitry Pichugin (b). Getty Images: Jamie Marshall— Tribaleye Images / The Image Bank (br). SuperStock: imagebroker.net (tl). 8–9 Alamy Images: Martin Harvey (b). 8 Dorling Kindersley: National Maritime Museum, London (tl). Robert Harding Picture Library: Last Refuge (br). 9 Alamy Images: Flavio Varricchio / BrazilPhotos (tl). Corbis: Ch'ien Lee / Minden Pictures (c). FLPA: Chien Lee / Minden Pictures (tr). PENGUIN and the Penguin logo are trademarks of Penguin Books Ltd: The lost World by Doyle, Arthur Conan, 2007. Cover reproduced with permission from Penguin Books Ltd. (br). 10–11 Dreamstime.com: Thomas Humeau (t). 10 Press Association Images: Norikazu Tateishi / AP (tr). 11 Dreamstime.com: Irina Drazowa-fischer (cra); Pondchao (tl). Getty Images: The Asahi Shimbun (cr). Photoshot: JTB (c). 12–13 Greg Willis (b). 13 123RF.com: lorcel (clb). Alamy Images: eye35.pix (rt); Ron Niebrugge (cra). Corbis: Stephanie Sawyer / Flickr (c). 14 Robert Harding Picture Library: Richard Ashworth (cla). 14–15 Alamy

Images: Jack Sullivan (c). 15 Alamy Images: Taylor S. Kennedy / National Geographic Image Collection (r). Corbis: Nathan Benn / Ottochrome (tr). Getty Images: Ilan Shacham / Flickr Open (cla); Keren Su / The Image Bank (br). 16 Dorling Kindersley: Hopi Learning Center, Arizona (tr). Getty Images: WIN-Initiative (cl). 16–17 Corbis: Kennan Ward (b). 17 Alamy Images: Robert Clay (c). Press Association Images: Tiffany Brown / AP (tr). 18 Alamy Images: Manfred Gottschalk (tr). 18–19 Dreamstime.com: Matthew Weinel (b). 19 Alamy Images: Bill Bachman (tl). Fotolia: Steve Lovegrove (tr). 20 Science Photo Library: Javier Trueba / Msf (cra). 20–21 Getty Images: Carsten Peter / Speleoresearch & Films / National Geographic (b). 21 Alamy Images: Bill Bachman (cl); Nic Cleave Photography (cr). Getty Images: Carsten Peter / Speleoresearch & Films / National Geographic (tr); Siede Preis / Photodisc (c). Science Photo Library: Dirk Wiersma (tr). 22–23 Alamy Images: Tom Gardner. 22 Alamy Images: M&G Therin-Weise / age fotostock (tr). Corbis: Kazuyoshi Nomachi (bc); George Steinmetz (cl). 23 Corbis: Atlantide Phototravel (tr). SuperStock: Biosphoto (bl). 24 Alamy Images: Sabena Jane Blackbird (clb). SuperStock: Biosphoto (c). 24–25 SuperStock: Life on White / Purestock (c). 25 Alamy Images: Ulrich Doering (clb); Erichui (br); Nolte Lourens (tr). 26 Alamy Images: McPHOTO / vario images (tr). Dreamstime.com: Luca Roggero (c). 26–27 SuperStock: age fotostock (t). 27 Corbis: Theo Allofs / Minden Pictures (t); Peter Johnson (cr). Photoshot: Imagebrokers (cl). 28 Corbis: Steven Vidler / Eurasia Press (b). Dreamstime.com: Petrsalinger (c). 28–29 Getty Images: Daniel Acevedo / age fotostock (t). 28–29 Getty Images: Michael Nichols / National Geographic (b). Robert Harding Picture Library: Christian Beier / CBpictures (tr). 30–31 123RF.com: Raweewat Tuntisavee (c). Oceanwideimages.com: (bc). 30 Dreamstime.com: Sburel (c). 31 Robert Harding Picture Library: Gonzalo Azumendi (ccl). 31 Dreamstime.com: Bgminer (c). Getty Images: David Doubilet / National Geographic (tr). 32 Alamy Images: Paul Springett A (c). Getty Images: Stephane De Sakutin / AFP (br). 32–33 Getty Images: Rob Verhoeven & Alessandra Magni / Flickr Open (c). 33 Alamy Images: David Wall (tl). Corbis: Splash News (br). Robert Harding Picture Library: Thomas

Dressler / age fotostock (tr). 34–35 Science Photo Library: Philippe Psaila (tl). 34 Corbis: Caroline Blumberg / Epa (tl). 35 Getty Images: Pierre Andrieu / AFP (tr); Mira Oberman / AFP (c); Dea / G. Dagli Orti (cr). 36 Corbis: David Nunuk / All Canada Photos (b). 37 Alamy Images: Adam Woolfitt / Robert Harding Picture Library Ltd (tr). Corbis: Richard T. Nowitz (cb). Dreamstime.com: Charlotte Leaper (tl). Getty Images: Glen Allison / Stone (bc); Image Hans Elbers / Flickr (c). 38 Robert Harding Picture Library: Robert Frerck / Odyssey (cla). Science Photo Library: David Nunuk (b). 38–39 Dreamstime.com: Jarnogz (b). 39 Alamy Images: Deco (br). Corbis: Bettmann (tl, br). Getty Images: Dea / G. Dagli Orti (cr). 40 The Bridgeman Art Library: Look and Learn (cr). SuperStock: Tips Images (bl). 41 Corbis: James L. Amos (cr); Kelly-Mooney Photography (clb). Dreamstime.com: Zhukovsky (br). Getty Images: Wojtek Buss / age fotostock (tr). 42 The Bridgeman Art Library: Brooklyn Museum of Art, New York, USA (cl). 42–43 Dreamstime.com: Danilo Mongiello (b). 43 Alamy Images: Deco (tr); Mireille Vautier (crb); Everett Collection Historical (br). 44 Alamy Images: Peter Horree (tr). 44–45 Alamy Images: Adrian Lyon (b). 45 akg-images: Jean-Louis Nou (cr). Alamy Images: Ancient Art and Architecture (cb); Davis James / Prisma Bildagentur AG (br). 46 Alamy Images: F1online digitale Bildagentur GmbH (bl). Getty Images: Apic / Hulton Archive (br). 47 akg-images: Jean-Louis Nou (bl). Alamy Images: Hans P. Szyszka / Novarc Images (c); Coninch, Salomon de (1609-74) (attr. to) / The Art Gallery Collection (tr). Getty Images: Photodisc / Alex Cao (bl). National Museum of Antiquities: Andreas F. Voegelin, Antikenmuseum Basel und Sammlung Ludwig / Department of Antiquities of Jordan (cla, cl/Oil lamp). Robert Harding Picture Library: Andrea Innocenti / Cubo Images (c). 48 Alamy Images: The Art Archive (cr); Liu Xiaoyang / China Images (cl). 48–49 Dreamstime.com: Mauhorng (Background); Sofiaworld (b). 49 Getty Images: STR / AFP (cr); Andrew Wong (c); Lane Oatey / Blue Jean Images (tr); Persian School / The Bridgeman Art Library (tl). 50 The Bridgeman Art Library: CNAM, Conservatoire National des Arts et Metiers, Paris / Archives Charmet (tl). Photo by yasa / Flickr Open (c); LL / Roger Viollet (br). 50–51 Dreamstime.com: Luciano Mortula (c). 51 Rex Features: Sipa Press (tl). SuperStock: F1 ONLINE (bl). 52 Getty Images: Dea / A. Jemolo (cl). 52–53 Dreamstime.com: Witr (c). Getty Images: Aladin Abdel Naby / Reuters (cr). Dreamstime.com: Mahmoud Mahdy (t). 54 Corbis: Araldo de Luca (tl). 54–55 Corbis: 145 (bc). Dreamstime.com: Mauhorng

(Background). 55 Corbis: Alinari Archives (cr); Michael Nicholson (c). Dorling Kindersley: Ermine Street Guard (cl/Military dagger). Getty Images: Dea / G. Dagli Orti (cl). 56 Dreamstime.com: Noelbynature (c); Oscar Espinosa Villegas (tr). 56–57 Alamy: Robert Harding World Imagery (b). 57 Corbis: Martin Puddy (cr). Dreamstime.com: Anil Grover (tr); Kjersti Joergensen (tl). 58–59 Getty Images: Gavin Hellier / Robert Harding World Imagery (b). 59 Alamy Images: Dinodia Photos RM (tl, tc). Corbis: Ocean (tr). Dreamstime.com: Shargaljut (cr). 60 Alamy Images: Witr (br); Sergio Pitamitz (cr). Corbis: Adam Woolfitt (cb, bl). Getty Images: Dea / A. Dagli Orti (tl). 61 Corbis: Markus Hanke / www.MarkusHanke.de (r). Getty Images: Dea / A. Dagli Orti (tl). 62–63 Dreamstime.com: Gilbert Agao (c). Getty Images: Xu Jian / The Image Bank (cla). Rex Features: Sipa Press (br). Photoshot: Al-Nakheel / Picture Alliance (b). Corbis: Ali Haider / Epa (tc). Dreamstime.com: Sippakorn Yamkasikorn (br). Photoshot: Al-Nakheel / Picture Alliance (b). Corbis: Ali Haider / Epa (tc). Dreamstime.com: Gilbert Agao (c). Getty Images: Xu Jian / The Image Bank (cla). Rex Features: Sipa Press (br). Corbis: Print Collector / Hulton Archive (cr). 64–65 Dreamstime.com: Lucasdm (Background). 65 The Bridgeman Art Library: Knab, Ferdinand (1834-1902) / Private Collection / Archives Charmet (tr). Corbis: Araldo de Luca (br); Charles & Josette Lenars (t). Getty Images: Culture Club / Hulton Archive (bl, bc). 66 Dorling Kindersley: Thomas Marent (br); Rough Guides (bl). Dreamstime.com: Dreamshot (tr). Getty Images: Carsten Peter / National Geographic (bc); Toshi Sasaki / Stone (cr). Science Photo Library: NOAA (c). 66–67 Dreamstime.com: Lucasdm (Background). 67 123RF.com: andreanita (bc). Corbis: Pete Oxford / Minden Pictures (tr). Dreamstime.com: Cosmopol (bc); Staphy (c); Josefhanus (tr); Paul Lemke (b). Getty Images: Steve Allen / Digital Vision (bc); GML / Flickr Open (tl). PunchStock: Digital Vision / Peter Adams (c). 68 Dreamstime.com: Ivan Sgualdini (br). Robert Harding Picture Library: Peter Langer / Insights (cr). 68–69 Dreamstime.com: Lucasdm (Background). 69 123RF.com: Daniel Haller (tr). Alamy Images: Gustav Gonget / G&B Images (br). Corbis: Uwe Zucchi / dpa (tl). Dorling Kindersley: Rough Guides (cla, tc/ Statue of Liberty). Getty Images: Carpe Feline / Flickr (br). Robert Harding Picture Library: David Poole (cb); Eitan Simanor (cb/Bethesda pool) (br). Getty Images: Angelo Hornak (cr). Corbis: Dea / A. Jemolo (b). 70–71 Dreamstime.com: Lucasdm (Background). 71 Dreamstime.com: Parnupong Norasethkamol (cr). Getty Images: Blanchot Philippe / Hemis.fr (tr)

All other images © Dorling Kindersley

For further information see: www.dkimages.com